D1177775

**DATE DUE**

| | | | |
|---|---|---|---|
| JA 13 91 | NO 4 '93 | | |
| FE 1 8 93 | | | |
| AE 18 '93 | | | |
| NO 24 '93 | | | |
| DE 5 '92 | | | |
| MY 3 0 '96 | | | |
| AG 1 '96 | | | |
| NO 18 '97 | | | |
| DE 19 '01 | | | |

# INVESTING
# IN
# CHILDREN

# INVESTING IN CHILDREN

## New Estimates of Parental Expenditures

Thomas J. Espenshade

*An Urban Institute Paperback*

 THE URBAN INSTITUTE PRESS · WASHINGTON, D.C.

**Library of Congress Cataloging in Publication Data**

Espenshade, Thomas J.
    Investing in children.

    Bibliography: p.
    1. Children—Economic aspects—United States.
2. Child rearing—Economic aspects—United States.
I. Title.
HQ792.U5E86   1984      339      84-5098
ISBN 0-87766-332-7

Printed in the United States of America

# Contents

# Tables

# FOREWORD

Current evidence suggests that parents vastly underestimate the amount of money they spend on their children. Of course, children do not come with price tags attached, but as all parents know, rearing children requires resources of time and money. This study by Thomas J. Espenshade provides new information on the level of money expenditures that parents, in various economic and demographic circumstances, make in rearing children. Expenditures vary according to parents' income and education, mother's employment status, and family size. The region of the country where a family lives, whether a family lives inside or outside a large metropolitan area, and the type of postsecondary education (if any) a child receives also affect parents' total expenditures.

Decision makers in both the public and private arenas will find such information valuable. For example, facts about the financial implications of parenthood can be included in parenthood education programs for high school students and other young adults. Furthermore, solid data on the financial aspects of childrearing may be useful in educational programs aimed at stemming the rise in out-of-wedlock births. For families affected by divorce, *Investing in Children* contains data helpful to the judicial system—as courts face the problem of setting fair amounts of child support. And, these data will help states draw up guidelines for reimbursing the foster care of children.

Finally, and perhaps most importantly, couples who are planning their families will welcome reliable information on what they can expect to spend on their children.

William Gorham
*President*
The Urban Institute

# ACKNOWLEDGMENTS

This research was conducted under contract with the Center for Population Research, National Institute of Child Health and Human Development (NICHD), Contract no. N01-HD-92824. NICHD project officers, Dr. Gloria Kamenske and Dr. V. Jeffery Evans, provided assistance and encouragement throughout this study. In addition, extensive conversations with Boone Turchi (University of North Carolina) have helped to sharpen the presentation. I am grateful to George Falco (Massachusetts Department of Social Services), Judith A. Hawes (National Center for State Courts), Margaret Malone (Congressional Research Service, Library of Congress), and Susan Paikin (Delaware Family Court) for the information they supplied. At The Urban Institute, Robert Meyer and Douglas Wolf made important contributions to the analysis. John Goodman, Jr., Lee Bawden, Robert Reischauer, and Shaun Murphy read the manuscript and offered helpful suggestions. Theresa Walker skillfully edited the final manuscript. My thanks are also extended to Thy Dao, John Moore, and Douglas Murray for their computer programming talents and to Carolyn O'Brien who assisted in the research. Bobbie Mathis rendered valuable technical service in typing the entire manuscript.

Finally, I wish to acknowledge a lasting intellectual debt to Kingsley Davis who first sparked my interest in this subject.

# ABOUT THE AUTHOR

Thomas J. Espenshade is a senior research associate in the Women and Family Policy Program at The Urban Institute. He received his Ph.D. in economics from Princeton University in 1972 and held research and teaching positions at the University of California (Berkeley), Bowdoin College, and Florida State University before joining the Institute in 1980. Dr. Espenshade's research interests include economic demography, population estimates and projections, marital behaviors of American men and women, and mathematical models of immigration processes. Among his publications are *The Cost of Children in Urban United States* (1976) and *The Economic Consequences of Slowing Population Growth* (1978).

# INVESTING
# IN
# CHILDREN

# 1

# *Introduction*

Rearing children requires expenditures of both time and money. Money expenditures consist of out-of-pocket direct maintenance expenses for items such as food, clothing, shelter, medical care, education, and other categories. Time or opportunity expenditures refer to the opportunities forgone by the time spent with children. These opportunity expenditures are perhaps less tangible, but no less important, and are often measured by the income the mother gives up by reducing her labor force participation below what it would be without children.

In 1980 I estimated that the sum of the direct and opportunity expenditures confronting American families varied on a per child basis from slightly more than $100,000 at the low-income level to nearly $140,000 for middle-income families (Espenshade 1980). These figures for 1980 were up about 30 percent over their corresponding 1977 levels. This study uses new data and an improved methodology to investigate the money expenditures that parents make on their children, and the following questions are addressed: (1) How much are parents likely to spend in rearing their children to age 18 or beyond? (2) How does this total vary according to the economic and demographic circumstances of families? and (3) Why are answers to these questions important?[1]

Persons wanting to know how much couples spend on their children often ask, "How much does it cost to raise a child?" In our opinion, however, asking about the *cost* of raising a child is unsatisfactory, not only because it invites answers that focus on some minimum level required for bio-

1

logical subsistence but also because the question implies a single answer when in fact a range of answers is possible. The following example clarifies the latter point. Suppose one asked, "What does it cost to own a car today?" Obviously, the answer depends on what kind of car one owns—old model versus new model, the cost of car insurance, the car's repair record, gas mileage, and the like. Thus, in this study, we distinguish between the concepts of cost and expenditure. We emphasize that we are estimating parental expenditures on children, not the cost of raising them. Our estimates of parental expenditures on children from the child's birth to age 18 vary depending on the parents' socioeconomic status (SES), number of children, and wife's employment status.

Information on what today's parents spend to rear their children has many practical uses. Most important, couples who are contemplating having children need a better sense of the financial responsibilities they will face as parents. Today when high interest rates may be forcing couples to decide between purchasing a home and starting a family, and when greater numbers of young people may feel that two incomes are necessary to support a suitable standard of living, parenthood education is especially critical. Furthermore, those who are already parents must be able to plan for the child-related expenses that await them down the road since children tend to become more expensive as they age. For example, parents may find that data on future expenditures on children are important to their financial planning in such areas as life insurance coverage and savings.

Information on parental expenditures on children is also needed to decide legal issues and various questions of public policy. For example, when couples with dependent children obtain a divorce, the issue of child support arises. Presumably, the level of child support should bear some relation to how much was being spent on the child(ren) in the previously intact family. And, attorneys are handling an increasing number of "wrongful birth" cases—cases, for example, where a couple did not want another child but had one owing to the alleged negligence of a physician (e.g., failure to perform an abortion, vasectomy, tubal ligation). In such cases, couples have sought to sue their doctor for malpractice and have asked that the damages include a sum sufficient to rear that child from birth to age 18. Finally, when deciding on appropriate funding levels for foster parents, states need to have guidelines on parental expenses on children.

## Overview and Summary

As stated earlier, our estimates of parental expenditures on children from the child's birth to age 18 exhibit great variation depending on the parents' socioeconomic status (SES), number of children, and wife's employment status. At the high end of the scale, per-child expenditures reach $135,700 (in 1981 prices) if couples from a high SES and in which the wife works full time, full year, have just one child. At the other extreme, we estimate that low SES families in which the wife does not work for pay and who have three children would commit an average of $58,300 per child in expenses to age 18. As a first approximation to the typical child in middle America, we may consider medium SES families with two children and a part-time working wife. In such families, parents are likely to spend $82,400 to rear a child to age 18.

Of the three factors—parents' SES, wife's employment status, and the number of children per family—number of children has the greatest impact on expenditures per child. To illustrate, consider again the $82,400 in per child expenditures in our prototypical middle-American family with two children, a medium SES, and a wife who works part time. Varying the number of children from one to three reduces per child expenditures from $106,200 to $68,800, or by 35 percent. Varying the couple's SES from high to low reduces per child expenditures from $98,300 to $75,000, or by 24 percent. Finally, comparing families where mothers work full time to families where mothers do no market work reduces per child expenditures from $94,100 to $76,400, or by 19 percent. Since expenditures per child are closely associated with children's (economic) welfare, parents may find that the most effective strategy for enhancing the material well-being of their children is to have smaller families.

Can a high SES and a full-time working mother offset the material disadvantages to children of growing up in a large family? Our results suggest that, within limits, the answer is yes. High SES families with three children would spend $87,600 per child if the wife works full time, and that total would be $89,500 in low SES families with one child if the mother is not employed outside the home.

Examining dollar expenditures on children does not by itself paint the whole picture of the economic responsibilities of parenthood because parents' ability to pay also varies. Perhaps a more complete view emerges when the percentage of total family consumption that represents expenditure on the children is analyzed. Our results show that this fraction varies remarkably little with a family's socioeconomic status but depends significantly on the number of children. Families with one child can expect to commit about 30 percent of total family expenditures to their child; in families with two children the proportion rises to between 40 and 45 percent; and in families with three children nearly 50 percent of total family spending is for the children.

For some families, the expenses involved with their children's college education may be the most significant outlay. Data from the College Entrance Examination Board show that, for the 1981–1982 academic year, annual expenses for higher education including tuition, room, and board ranged between $3,230 for a typical public two-year college and $6,885 for an average private four-year institution. Consequently, when the cost of postsecondary education is figured in, our previous estimates could be increased by anywhere between $6,460 (two years at a public institution) and $27,540 (four years at a private college or university). If we assume that a child from middle America will attend a four-year public college or university (estimated cost equals $15,492), the total estimated expenditure from birth to college graduation approaches $100,000.

As children age they tend to become more expensive. If we divide the first 18 years of a child's life into three equal age groups, in general we find that approximately 26 percent of total child-related expenditures to age 18 arise at ages 0–5, and roughly equal amounts occur at ages 6–11 (36 percent) and 12–17 (38 percent). These age-group shares tend to vary with the birth order of the child in the family. Because the economies of scale related to having more than one child are concentrated under age 6, the second child's expenses in a two-child family are more heavily weighted toward the older years. When all 18 years are combined, we find that despite the existence of economies of scale in childrearing, they are not large; savings of 5 to 10 percent of expenditures on the previous child are usually identified with each additional child.

Besides presenting results for the entire United States, our study examines black-white differences in child-related expenditure patterns, as well as differences connected with residence in particular regions of the country and with living inside or outside large urban areas. We find, for instance, that white families generally spend more on their children than do comparable black families, although the differences are not striking. A white family at the medium SES level with two children and a wife who works full time spends an average of $93,850 per child from birth to age 18, compared to $91,000 per child in black families with similar characteristics. In general, more seems to be spent in rearing children in the Northeast and West than in either the South or the North Central census regions. And families living in metropolitan areas spend more on children than families in nonmetropolitan areas. For example, for families with two children, a medium SES background, and a wife who works full time, per child expenditures are estimated to be $98,700 inside standard metropolitan statistical areas (SMSAs) and $83,500 outside SMSAs.

We have disaggregated expenditures on children to age 18 into seven major categories of consumption including food, clothing, housing, transportation, recreation, medical care, and miscellaneous. Transportation (25.1 percent of the total), housing (24.1 percent), and food (22.5 percent) are typically the three most important budget items for children, and when these expenses are combined they make up nearly three-fourths of the total.

Parents' plans to have children may include decisions about the timing and spacing of children as well as the number. What help can our estimates provide to couples confronted with these decisions? First, our estimates show that expenditures on children appear to be relatively insensitive to the birth interval separating them. Even though lengthening the birth interval from one year to four years tends to increase expenditures per child, the increase is less than 5 percent. For example, in middle-American families, expenditures rise from $81,300 per child when one year separates the two children, to $84,750 per child when the birth interval is four years. Second, our previous estimates assumed that mothers are 25 years old when their first child is born. What difference would it make if we assumed mothers to be 22, 27, or 32 years old? Delayed childbearing increases expenditures on children, but the difference is noteworthy only for high SES families. Expenditures per child by parents with a high SES background are 9.3 percent larger when mothers begin childbearing at age 32 than if they begin at age 22 ($102,700 per child versus $94,000 per child). At the medium and low SES levels, expenditures rise by just 3.6 and 2.5 percent, respectively. Our overall conclusion here is that, for couples considering having children, choices regarding the number of children will vastly outweigh the effects of timing and spacing insofar as parental expenditures per child are concerned.

Data from the U.S. Department of Agriculture (USDA) are often cited as a source of estimates of parental expenditures on children. Despite differences in data bases and in approach, the USDA's estimates are close to ours in terms of both the total estimated expenditure to age 18 and the age distribution of that total. We find that the average American family spends $82,400 per child, compared to the USDA's estimate of $80,400, and our numbers for the proportionate breakdown into the age groups 0-5, 6-11, and 12-17 are 26, 36, and 38 percent, respectively, versus 29, 33, and 38 percent from the USDA's figures. However, because of differences in data and in estimation procedures, the USDA shows housing to constitute over one-third (34 percent) of the total expenditure to age 18, and transportation makes up just 15 percent. Moreover, we find sharp evidence that a family's living standard varies over the life cycle and is not constant as the USDA assumes. In two-child families, for example, living standards start to fall with the birth of the first child, reach a low point when the two children are age 10 and 8, and then begin a slow but gradual rise until the children reach the end of their teenage years.

The estimates we have just described are cast in 1981 prices. What can a family anticipate in future expenditures if their first child is born in 1981 and if we factor future inflation into the estimates? Under the low-inflation scenario, which assumes an annual rate of inflation of 5.2 percent, expenditures to age 18 in our two-child middle-American family rise from $82,400 per child in constant 1981 dollars to $149,000 per child in projected future dollars. At the medium-inflation level (8.0 percent per annum), our estimate of future expenditures reaches $200,000 per child; and with the high-inflation scenario (9.3 percent per annum) the total climbs to $228,000 per child. Moreover, accounting for anticipated college costs could boost the expense of rearing a child from birth through four years of college to between $196,000 and $310,000, depending on the type of four-year institution and the assumption regarding future inflation.

## Applications

Information on how much parents are spending to rear their children has practical application in several areas, including education for parenthood, setting child support awards, and determining allowances for foster children.

## Parenthood Education

Constructing estimates of parental expenditures on children gives couples more accurate information about the financial responsibilities of parenthood. Unfortunately, current evidence suggests that most people are grossly misinformed about the economic liabilities of rearing children. For example, in a Value of Children survey conducted in Hawaii by Fred Arnold and James Fawcett (1976), couples were asked, "About how much money in all do you think it has cost you to raise your children over the last twelve months?" Urban middle-class Caucasian parents perceived that child-related expenditures accounted for just 14.7 percent of yearly income. These amounts are consistently below estimates of actual out-of-pocket expenses produced in an earlier study (see Espenshade 1973). There, middle-income parents are estimated to spend an average of 40.7 percent of annual income on two children to raise them to age 18.[2]

As helpful as the numbers in this study may be for planning purposes, they should not be interpreted as applying perfectly to the circumstances of each and every family. They are only an effort to capture average tendencies for families of particular types, and inevitably there are variations around the mean. Some families will spend more and some less than the figures shown in chapter 4. Nevertheless, any discrepancies between these numbers and the unique circumstances of individual families are likely to be substantially less than the gulf currently separating parents' perceptions of expenditures on their children and independent estimates of those expenditures.

## Child Support Awards

Another use for data on how much parents are spending on their children is to aid courts in setting child support awards. One can argue that, whether the ultimate size of the award is arrived at through the application of a strict formula or through more flexible guidelines, it should bear some relation to the child's level of consumption before the divorce.

Currently, there appears to be considerable variability in how judges set amounts for child support. Some states have attempted to develop model statutes, whereas in others judges are permitted wide discretion. Michigan law, for example, sets forth no specific formula for fixing orders of child support. According to David Chambers (1979), "Like statutes in many states, the Michigan statute authorizing courts to enter orders for child support gives the court no guidance whatever" (p. 38). The court, at the time of granting the divorce, is empowered to make "such further decree as it shall deem just and proper concerning the...maintenance of the minor children of the parties" (Chambers, 1979: 38–39), but judges have no other guidelines.

To fill this vacuum, Michigan's local judges have developed their own informal schedules for setting child support. In nearly all counties, the size of the award depends on just two factors: the number of children in the family and the net earnings (after taxes and Social Security) of the noncustodial parent. In the twenty-eight counties surveyed in Michigan, Chambers (1979) found that orders of support ranged between 18 and 23 percent of a father's net earnings if only one child was involved in the divorce, and between 45 and 48 percent of a father's income was set for four children.[3]

Perhaps the most interesting aspect of the schedules commonly used in Michigan is how they arose out of everyday practice. According to Chambers (1979), "None of the schedules, so far as we can learn, were developed after a study of the actual costs of raising children or after determining the earnings of working mothers" (p. 40). Apparently, the situation in other states is similar. Chambers (1979) observes, "In many places, no child-support schedule is used, the statutory language is as cloudy as Michigan's, and lawyers bargain over child support in each case as part of a common package that includes alimony and the division of real and personal property" (p. 40).[4]

Despite the apparent haphazard nature by which child support is meted out, some states stand out for their exemplary and systematic approaches to the problem. In the state of Delaware, for example, the family court adopted the Melson formula in 1979 and applies it to between 80 and 85 percent of the divorce cases involving minor children. More than a series of calculations, the Melson formula conceptualizes how Delaware looks at child support. Both parents are equally obligated for the support of minor children. Thus, the incomes of both parents are relevant. Other factors considered include living arrangements (who has custody and whether joint custody is awarded), the number of children, and whether either parent has remarried. As part of the Melson formula's application, minimum support needs for children are established. The amounts are $400 per month for a first child, $160 per month for a second child, and $120 per month for third and higher-order births.

According to Susan Paikin in the Family Court of Delaware, many states are trying to move away from the mood of the judge by developing basic information of the "where the lines cross" type.[5] For example, in Virginia, a matrix is used to determine the suggested minimum child support payment by matching the monthly adjusted gross income of the absent parent with the number of dependents in the absent parent's present family and the locality of the absent parent's residence. Other examples of where straight guidelines are being applied include Chester and Allegheny counties in Pennsylvania. The Melson formula in Delaware has been adopted by Wisconsin, and both Iowa and Oregon have also adopted systematic procedures. Nevertheless, as suggested by this brief sketch, the room for improvement is still large in many states. If children are not going to have to share in the decreased standard of living necessarily resulting from the costs of maintaining one parent in separate quarters, then procedures for awarding child support must incorporate information on children's consumption in their previously intact family.

## Foster Care

In the area of foster care, a key issue is the determination of how much foster parents should be reimbursed for the care they give to foster children.

TABLE 1    Family Foster Care Reimbursement Rates in Selected States and
Metropolitan Areas, 1981

| State or Area | Basic Monthly Allowance | Relevant Age Group of Children |
|---|---|---|
| Alabama | $171 | 6–12 |
| Connecticut | 178 | 6–11 |
| Georgia | 143 | 6–11 |
| Los Angeles | 310 | 5–8 |
| Los Angeles | 343 | 9–11 |
| Maine | 152 | 5–11 |
| Massachusetts | 182 | 7–12 |
| Mississippi | 123 | 7–12 |
| Missouri | 150 | 6–12 |
| New Hampshire | 121 | — |
| New Jersey | 171 | 6–9 |
| New York metropolitan area | 216 | 6–11 |
| Pennsylvania | 235 | 5–11 |
| Rhode Island | 160 | 0–12 |
| Vermont | 175 | 6–12 |
| West Virginia | 125 | 5–8 |

SOURCE: Lauderdale, Anderson, Spiegel (1981).

Data on parental expenditures on children are directly relevant, especially if they are disaggregated by the birth order of the child since foster children tend often to complement one's family of natural children.

Shown in table 1 are data from a study by Lauderdale, Anderson, and Spiegel (1981) reflecting basic monthly allowances for foster children in 1981. Not all areas the authors surveyed are shown in table 1, but we have included those at both the high end (Pennsylvania, New York metropolitan area, and Los Angeles) and low end (New Hampshire, West Virginia, and Mississippi) of the scale. According to George Falco of the Massachusetts Department of Social Services, most progressive states (including Massachusetts) try to assume the full reimbursement costs of foster care.[6] If this is the case, then the data in table 1, together with the estimates presented in chapter 4, suggest that most, if not all, states fall short of this goal. For example, our estimates in chapter 4, which are also for calendar year 1981, show that middle SES parents can expect to spend approximately $64,700 on a third child in a three-child family to rear that child to age 18. Dividing that total first by eighteen and then again by twelve to reflect an average monthly expenditure yields $300 per month. By this measure, most states do not fully reimburse parents for the cost of the foster care they provide.

# 2

# Review of Related Studies

As stated earlier, expenditures by parents on their children generally have two components: (1) direct maintenance expenditure, that is, the out-of-pocket expenses for such items as food, clothing, housing, education, and medical care and (2) opportunity expenditure, or the opportunities parents typically forgo when they bear and raise children. Some of the research on expenditures on children has attempted to quantify both the direct and opportunity expenditures (see Reed and McIntosh 1972; Turchi 1975; and Espenshade 1977, 1980). Although we include several of these studies in this review, our discussion of the findings will generally be limited to those that deal specifically with the direct money expenditures on children.

Interest in estimating expenditures on children dates as far back as the nineteenth century. An appraisal of the various methodological practices that had been employed before 1972 is included in works by Espenshade (1972, 1973). Among the studies reviewed there are ones by Engel (1883, 1887, 1895), Ogburn (1919), Dublin and Lotka (1946), Pennock (1970a, 1970b), Mork (1966), Sohn (1970), Henderson (1949-1950), and Nicholson (1949).

In a more recent attempt at estimating parental expenditures on children, Espenshade (1973) modified Henderson's methodology and applied this new framework to data from the Bureau of Labor Statistics' (BLS) 1960-1961 Survey of Consumer Expenditures (SCE). Estimates of expenditures on children to age 18 were detailed by family income, family size,

11

age of child, birth order, and by category of expenditure (including food, housing, clothing, transportation, medical, insurance, gifts, a category called "net saving," and miscellaneous other). This new method avoided two unrealistic yet common assumptions found in previous methods: (1) that expenses are independent of the birth order of the child in the family and (2) that living standards are constant when children are growing up.

Findings from this study indicate that the first child in a family is likely to be more expensive than subsequent children, with the marginal cost of the first child often being as much as twice that of a second child. Second and third children were found about equally expensive. Additionally, expenditures on children tend to increase with the age of the child, with three times as much being spent on a child between the ages of 12 and 17 compared to that spent for a child between ages 0 and 5. Food, housing, and clothing are the most important expenditure items in the child's budget.

A study for the 1970–1972 U.S. Commission on Population Growth and the American Future prepared by Ritchie Reed and Susan McIntosh (1972) provided estimates of the size of the direct expenses confronting American parents in 1969. Their figures are based on USDA estimates for expenditures on children that in turn were derived from the 1960–1961 SCE and then inflated to reflect 1969 prices.[1] Reed and McIntosh presented estimates for the monetary outlays needed to maintain an *average* child in a family of husband and wife with two to five children. The authors estimated expenditures for two alternative income levels and prepared separate calculations for the expenses of childbirth, other maintenance costs to age 18, and the cost of a four-year college education. In addition, these totals were tabulated for single years of age, by four regions of the United States, and for farm, rural nonfarm, and urban residents. Findings revealed that the outlays typically linked with raising an urban child from birth through four years of college ranged from $27,109 at the low cost level to $39,924 at the moderate cost level, in 1969 prices.

To provide a more up-to-date picture of the direct money expenditures parents make in bearing and rearing their children through the completion of college, Espenshade (1977) prepared new estimates using these same USDA data. For the sake of comparability the methodology developed by Reed and McIntosh was repeated here, but Consumer Price Index (CPI) information was used to bring the data up to 1977 prices. These figures pointed out that the family's standard of living is the most important determinant of child-related purchases. Espenshade's estimates for the total expenditures on children at the moderate cost level ($64,215) are approximately 50 percent more than those at the low cost level ($44,156). Housing was the most costly item in total child-rearing expenditures, followed by food and transportation.

These figures were updated again by Espenshade (1980) to reflect the dramatic rise in the CPI between 1977 and 1980. Each expenditure component was inflated separately using disaggregated CPI data and then recombined to produce a total estimate for direct expenditures in 1980 prices. Estimates for the total direct expenses for a child at the moderate cost level rose to $85,163, including four years of college—an increase of 33 percent since 1977.

Using data from two separate surveys, Edwards (1981) estimates average annual and total expenditures on children from birth to age 18 for eight separate expense categories, by census region, place of residence, and cost level. Estimates for urban and rural nonfarm families are based on the 1960-1961 SCE, and the estimates for farm families are derived from the USDA's 1973 Farm Family Living Expenditure Survey. Updated to reflect June 1981 prices, the USDA's (1982) estimate for the total expenditures required to raise an urban child from birth to age 18 at the moderate cost level in the North Central region is $75,736. An important limitation of this study's approach is its assumption that the family's standard of living remains constant over the period that the children are in the household, an assumption contradicted by other research. Further, the fact that expenditure patterns have changed since the 1960-1961 Survey of Consumer Expenditures was conducted raises questions about the reliability of estimates for 1981 based on these older data.

Using a different approach, Turchi (1975) utilized data from the 1960-1961 SCE, the 1965 Productive Americans Survey, and the 1970 Family Economics Survey to estimate money expenditures on children through the completion of college for each of six potential income groups. Expenditures were itemized for food, clothing, recreation, housing, and education and were presented for several age categories of the children. The list of expenditure categories was not an exhaustive one, however, and the use of multiple data sources in estimating the several components of total expenses creates some problems in comparability.

Turchi's estimates for the total expenses on children for these five expenditure categories, in 1969 prices, range from $8,947 for the lowest potential income group to $18,728 for the highest group. Differences in estimated educational expenses account for much of the variation among groups. These figures are much lower than other comparable findings, even when they have been inflated to include the missing expenditure categories.

In more recent work, Turchi (1979) presents new estimates of the expenditures required to raise a child in the United States, again based on the 1960–1961 Survey of Consumer Expenditures. Actual expenditures on children from birth to age 18 are developed for each of ten commodity groups. Age profiles of expenditure are shown for each of the commodity groups, and an aggregate expenditure profile is computed. In addition, differences in the expense of a child by economic status groups are shown. The methodology used in developing these estimates proceeds directly from the economic theory of consumer choice, allowing an assessment of the relative importance of both economic and noneconomic factors in determining the dollar cost of a child.

Turchi's new estimate of the average cumulative expenditures for a child from birth to age 18 is $20,320, in 1960–1961 prices. Food expenditures, accounting for more than 30 percent of the total expenditures on a child, again constitute the largest expense for parents, followed by housing, with a 22–24 percent share, and clothing with a 17 percent share. Turchi's research supports other findings that indicate that children become more expensive as they age. In this study, 17 percent of the total expenses are incurred in the first six years, 32 percent in the next six years, and 51 percent in the final six years.

In a monumental undertaking, Lindert (1978) developed an index of the *relative* cost of a child. This index supplies measures of the variation in the expenditures on American children over time and across groups. Its relevance to this study, however, is somewhat tangential since the relative cost of an extra child is defined simply as the ratio of two price indices. In other words, we end up not with a dollar figure but simply with a number that reflects temporal variations in relative prices. Moreover, the index takes into account inputs of both commodities (i.e., the direct expenditures on children) and time (i.e., the opportunity expenditures on children).

Lazear and Michael (1980) have considered the problem of how to make standard of living comparisons among families differing in size and composition. Equating standard of living with real per capita income, they estimate the economies of scale implicit in household expenditure patterns. Their estimates contain implications for describing money expenditures on children, but Lazear and Michael do not attempt to quantify these costs. However, using their data, it is possible to show that, provided family income remains fixed, living standards decline as the number of children increases, with the first child having the greatest impact (a 17.3 percent reduction). The combined effect of adding the second and third child is only slightly greater than the addition of the first child alone. Moreover, for a family of five, consisting of husband, wife, and three children, the Lazear-Michael data imply that 37.2 percent of total family consumption could be accounted for by the children. The remaining 62.8 percent would be adult consumption, with the husband's share comprising 59.2 percent and the wife's 3.6 percent. These findings imply substantial economies of scale in household consumption, especially for the wife.

Recently van der Gaag (1982) completed a study that compares the various approaches used in the past to estimate the total expenditures on children. He concludes that the majority of this work falls into two distinct categories: (1) the indirect methods, or those that use observed household consumption patterns as the basis of their analysis and (2) the direct methods, or techniques that use information obtained directly through surveys to measure individual welfare functions of income. Both approaches produce levels of well-being that are then used to measure total spending on children. Van der Gaag also discusses the importance of various household characteristics often ignored in the analysis of expenditures on children, for example, age of the household, parents' ages, and parents' employment status.

A more recent study by Olson (1982) provides estimates on the expenses of childrearing based on more up-to-date data from the 1972–1973 Consumer Expenditure Survey (CES). Expenditures are allocated between adults and children through comparing differences in the relationship between expenditures on observable adult goods (alcohol, tobacco, and adult clothing) and total expenditures in families without children and those with children. Estimates of total expenses are presented for children born in 1980 by sex, race, age, number of children in the family, and level of family income. Olson also supplies estimates for net expenditures or the level of parental expenditures on the children, net of children's contributions to family income. Using a model that allows for changes in family income over time, estimates of expenditures on children for six cost categories are projected under three different inflation scenarios. Olson's findings show that an average two-parent family with no previous children, head age 25, can expect to spend $202,878 in undiscounted 1980 dollars to raise a son born in 1980 from birth to age 22, allowing for four years of private college. Expenditures for food consume the largest share of the total child-rearing budget, followed by housing and transportation.

Bentley, Ofori-Mensa, Ransom, and Wise (1981) use a household expenditures approach to forecast the cost of children from birth to age 18, under several scenarios regarding future inflation. Household expenditure functions for sixteen categories of family structure, differing in age, number, and spacing of children, are compared with a childless reference family. Total expenses are computed separately by race, census region, and expenditure level for each of seven commodity groups. Some of the results from this study contradict previous findings in the literature on parental expenditures on children. For instance, the figures say that the expenses involved in raising a single child decline with age, and the same pattern appears for households with more than one child. The significance of this finding, however, is somewhat diminished because this computation does not include expenditures on education.

Recent interest in documenting the size and distribution of intrafamily transfers has produced some information relevant to the research on parental expenditures on children. Using data from the Panel Study of Income Dynamics, Morgan (1978) computed estimates of intrafamily transfers by age and sex, using different assumptions regarding the dollar value of housework and child care. These figures demonstrate that intrafamily transfers from birth to age 17 total $19,839 and $19,248 for sons and daughters, respectively. These estimates are net of any contributions to family income by children. Additional work on intrafamily transfers by Lillydahl and Sindell (1982) also discusses the long-range implications of varying investments in children.

Finally, although such studies do not provide specific estimates of total expenditures on children, theoretical studies on the allocation of resources by parents may be important for this topic. Behrman, Pollak, and Taubman (1982) have developed a preference model for analyzing the allocation of resources among children. The findings disclose that parents are more likely to spend more on the less able child. Sheshinski and Weiss (1982) also discuss the relationship between differences in children's ability and the distribution of expenditures within and between families.

# 3

# *Data and Methods*

In this chapter we give an overview of the data and methods used to produce the expenditure estimates reported in chapter 4. (The appendix contains a more complete discussion of methodology.) First, however, we summarize briefly the novel features of the analysis of parental expenditures on children.

## New Features of the Analysis

There are at least eight new features of this analysis which, when taken together, mark a significant advance over earlier estimates. First, more recent data are used for consumer incomes and expenditures. Second, variations in the wife's employment status are permitted to affect child-related purchases. Third, differences in the timing and spacing of births are included along with the number of children in a more comprehensive examination of childbearing patterns. Fourth, black-white differences in spending behaviors are studied. Fifth, expenditure estimates are given for each child in a family so that economies of scale can be assessed. Sixth, family living standards fluctuate in a realistic fashion while children are at home. Seventh, information on college costs is included in the estimates. Finally, two general kinds of estimates are produced: (1) those based on constant 1981 dollars and (2) those that incorporate alternative assumptions about the magnitude of inflation beyond 1981.

17

# Data

Data for this study come from the 1972–1973 Consumer Expenditure Survey (CES) conducted by the U.S. Bureau of the Census on behalf of the U.S. Bureau of Labor Statistics (BLS). These data are the most recent and most comprehensive information on family expenditures and income related to socioeconomic and demographic characteristics of U.S. families, replacing those data collected in the BLS 1960–1961 *Survey of Consumer Expenditures* (SCE).

The 1972–1973 survey consists of two separate parts: (1) a diary survey in which respondents recorded their expenditures for two 1-week periods and (2) an interview panel survey in which families reported information to interviewers at three-month intervals over a fifteen-month period. The interview portion, on which our analysis is based, covered the calendar years 1972 and 1973 and included 9,869 sample consumer units in 1972 and 10,106 different consumer units in 1973.

The 1972–1973 CES is a national sample survey covering both urban and rural portions of the United States. The eligible population included the civilian noninstitutional population as well as that portion of the institutional population living in rooming or boarding houses or living in doctors' and nurses' quarters of general hospitals. Armed forces personnel living outside military installations were included in the coverage, but armed forces personnel living on post were excluded.

Data in the 1972–1973 survey were collected from consumer units (CUs) defined as (1) a group of two persons or more, usually living together, who pool their income and draw from a common fund for major items of expense or (2) a person living alone or sharing a household with others, or living as a roomer in a private home, lodging house, or hotel, but who is financially independent, that is, the person's income and expenditures are not pooled with those of other residents.

Our working file was created by merging information from the Interview Survey Summary Public Use Tape and the Interview Survey Detailed Public Use Tape No. 2.[1] In general, information on total current consumption expenditures and its components (e.g., food at home, food away from home, shelter, fuel and utilities, and the like) was obtained from the summary public use tape. All other information, including household income, socioeconomic, and demographic characteristics, was taken from the detailed tape no. 2. This version of the detailed public use tape eliminates some top- and bottom-coding present in earlier editions. Affected variables include family size, number of automobiles owned, market value and rental value of owned home, income, personal taxes, and ages of family members.

Not all CUs in the interview survey have been selected for inclusion in our analysis. To be chosen, CUs had to be the husband-wife type. Moreover, husband-wife families were restricted to those containing either no other persons or just children of the husband and wife. All children had to be under 25 years of age, and all husbands in husband-wife-only families had to be under 55 years of age. Finally, households were excluded if they had occupied the dwelling unit for less than the full survey year, or if they refused to report or had incomplete reporting on income. After all these exclusions, we were left with 8,547 consumer units in our sample. For the purpose of analysis, data from the two survey years were combined, including 4,284 CUs from 1972 and 4,263 from 1973.

## Methods

In estimating the level of expenditures parents make in rearing their children the central problem is apportioning total family consumption to individual family members. Two elements contribute to the difficulty. First, income and expenditure data such as those found in the 1972–1973 CES are usually collected at the household level and not separately for individuals. For example, expenditures by family members on food consumed away from home in restaurants are, in principle, assignable to individuals, but most surveys simply report a single annual dollar figure for the household unit. Second, other items such as shelter expenses are conceptually difficult to assign to particular family members. Since all family members presumably consume services provided by a kitchen or a living room (but the level of consumption may vary across family members), how does one apportion shelter costs to individuals?

These twin problems may be resolved in several ways. The approach we adopt here is to develop an index of a family's material standard of living and then to apply this index to a comparison of the living standards of families that may differ substantially in income, consumption, and family size and composition.[2] Specifically, we have elected to use as our measure of a family's material standard of living the percentage of total current consumption expenditure devoted to food consumed at home (PFDHM). Moreover, we assume that two families with the same value for PFDHM have the same standard of living, regardless of other differences with respect either to the volume of total consumption or to family size and/or composition.

Providing data for parenthood education is a main goal of this study. To achieve that goal, we must define prototypical families with which couples can identify. Because families differ with regard both to socioeconomic characteristics of husbands and wives (education, occupation, employment status) and to such demographic characteristics as family size and child spacing, the potential number of prototypical families we could consider surpasses manageable limits. Therefore, some way is needed to reduce this number and to select those family types most likely to arise in practice.

To focus the analysis, we will present results for only three levels of socioeconomic status (SES). Families with a high SES are those in which the husband has some college education and a white-collar job. Medium SES families are characterized by husbands with a high school diploma and a blue-collar occupation. Husbands with less than a high school education and a blue-collar job fall into the low SES group. We will assume further that wives have the same educational attainment as their husbands. In presenting the estimates, we will limit our discussion to wives who either do no market work at all outside the home or who work all year (either full time or part time). Thus, each of the three socioeconomic status categories can be paired with one of three employment status categories for the wife, giving us a total of nine family types differentiated by socioeconomic characteristics. Of course, besides socioeconomic characteristics, families also differ according to demographic circumstances, including the total number of children ever born, the spacing (in years) between successive births, a mother's age at first birth, and the difference between the husband's age and the wife's age.

We will sometimes use the term *family income* to refer to socioeconomic status as if the two were synonymous. In fact, this is not the case. We deliberately chose relatively time-invariant factors such as education and occupation to characterize socioeconomic status. Within each SES category, however, income is not constant. It varies over the life cycle according to age-earnings profiles of husbands and wives. In addition, family income depends upon a wife's employment status and on where a family lives (whether in a metropolitan or nonmetropolitan area and in which part of the country). Therefore, by fixing a family's socioeconomic bracket, we are assuming that the household head's education and broad occupational category remain constant, although family income may fluctuate in response to changes in the husband's age or in either the wife's age or employment status. (Refer to Table A.12 for an empirical example of how income varies within each SES category.)

We will identify each of our prototypical families by assigning to them values for each of these six parameters (two parameters for socioeconomic characteristics and four parameters for demographic characteristics). For example, we may be interested in estimating the accumulated total of parental expenditures on children up to age 18 in a family with a high SES background, with a mother who works full time all year, and with two children spaced two years apart, the elder of whom is born when the mother is 25 years old and the father is 27 years old.

To produce estimates of parental expenditures on children within particular family types, we construct a synthetic life cycle for the family, beginning with the year in which the first child is born. For each year that there are children in the household we estimate the husband's and wife's earnings, total family consumption, and the percentage of total family consumption allocated to food at home (PFDHM). Application of our standard-of-living (SOL) equation (table A.15) permits us then to distribute total family consumption to the parents and to each of the children.

To illustrate the estimation strategy let us return to the family just described and consider this family in the year in which the older child is 10 years old and the younger is age 8. In that year, the mother will be 35 and the father will be 37 years old. The husband's earnings depend on his age, education (college), and occupation (white collar). On this basis we can estimate his yearly earnings at $17,692 (in 1972–1973 prices). Similarly, the wife's earnings of $8,101 can be estimated from her age and education (assumed to be the same as her husband's). Total family consumption is assumed to be a function of the family's size and age composition and of the husband's and wife's earnings. Since the ages of all family members are known, total family spending can be estimated as $12,220.

Now we want to know how much of this consumption is attributable to the parents and how much to the 10- and 8-year-old children. Application of our SOL equation to this family implies that the family, given its total consumption and its family size and composition, would devote 16.9 percent of its total current consumption expenditure to food at home. We must ask what level of total current consumption would produce the same share allocated to food at home if the husband and wife had no children. To answer this question we solve the SOL equation in table A.15 for the value of C, given that PFDHM = 16.9 and that the family consists of just two persons, one age 37 and the other age 35. Solving this way for C implies that a childless couple would require a total annual consumption of $6,091 to maintain the same standard of living as the two-child family whose total spending is $12,220. We then infer that the difference of $6,129 (= 12,220 − 6,091) is the expenditure on the children required to bring them up to the same standard of living as the adults.

To divide total child-oriented expenditures of $6,129 into expenditures on the first (i.e., elder) child and on the second, we ask how much consumption a family consisting of father (age 37), mother (age 35), and one child (age 10) would require to devote a 16.9 percent share to food at home. Again solving the SOL equation for C, we find that $9,143 is the needed amount. That calculation then implies that of the $6,129 expended on both children together, $3,052 ( = 9,143 − 6,091) is the estimated consumption by the 10-year-old child and the remainder, or $3,077 ( = 12,220 − 9,143), is the estimated expenditure on the second child. Procedures identical to these are followed to estimate expenditures on children at other points in the family life cycle, and, therefore, for other ages of children.

A final word of explanation is needed concerning how we disaggregate annual expenditures on each child into expenditures for shelter, transportation, medical care, and other categories. Using the equations in table A.13 that describe the pattern of total family spending, we can estimate how much the two-child family with total annual consumption of $12,220 and two children (ages 10 and 8) would spend, say, for shelter. We have already determined that a childless couple would need $6,091 in total consumption to maintain the same standard of living without the children, and application of the shelter equation in table A.13 predicts how much the childless couple would spend for shelter. The difference between the predicted shelter expenditures for the two-child family with total annual expenses of $12,220 and the childless couple with total annual expenses of $6,091 is the estimated shelter expenditure *on the two children combined*. These expenses may be allocated to the children individually by estimating the shelter expenditures for a family with one child (age 10) and total annual consumption of $9,143. Similar procedures would be used to infer child-oriented expenditures on other categories of consumption. Because we have used the same specification in table A.13 for each expenditure item, we are assured that the separately estimated components of expenditures (shelter, etc.) on a child at a given age add up identically to total expenditures on that child at that age.[3]

# 4

# Results of the Analysis

In this chapter we present our principal findings. We give estimates of the level of parental expenditures involved in rearing children to age 18, including the cost of a college education when that is a consideration, for families in various socioeconomic and demographic circumstances. Our estimates to age 18 are broken down into three categories: under 6, 6–11, and 12–17. Not all children become financially independent at age 18, and indeed our estimates account for the possibility that children may be consumer unit members until age 25. Nevertheless, in many families children are financially dependent at least until age 18, so that by presenting estimates up to that age we can set a lower bound on anticipated expenditures.

The data for this study were collected in 1972 and 1973, but given the inflation in the United States between 1972–1973 and the writing of this report, estimates expressed in 1972–1973 prices would not be reliable under current conditions. Therefore, for the most part, the figures we discuss in this chapter are updated from 1972–1973 and expressed in terms of 1981 price levels. (At the time the inflation updates were being prepared, Consumer Price Index (CPI) data for 1982 were not yet available from the Bureau of Labor Statistics (BLS).)

The procedures used for making inflation adjustments between 1972–1973 and 1981 are as follows. Our methodology for computing expenditures on children calculates, for each year that children are in the household, the total expenditure on each child and the disaggregation of

that total expenditure into ten separate categories of consumption, expressed in 1972–1973 prices. Rather than apply the universal increase in
the CPI between 1972–1973 and 1981 to our estimates of parental expenditures on children, we examined the category-specific rates of inflation
between 1972–1973 and 1981, applied those rates to 1972–1973 estimates
of expenditures to age 18 in particular categories of consumption, and
then recombined the results for 1981. Table 2 shows the item-specific
rates of inflation between 1972–1973 and 1981 for each of our ten
categories of consumption. Clothing prices increased the least over this
period—by 48.6 percent. At the other extreme, prices for fuel and utilities
in 1981 were 162.7 percent above their average level for 1972–1973. To
bring the estimates described here up to the level of prices prevailing in
1984 or later, readers may follow a similar procedure and apply category-
specific rates of inflation between 1981 and the desired year (these are
published monthly in the BLS *Monthly Labor Review*) to the estimates
shown in tables 14, 15, and 16.

The procedures we have used to inflate our results to 1981 prices allow for changes in relative prices over the period in question because different rates of inflation are used for each commodity group. As mentioned, clothing prices increased in absolute terms over the period, but
since the prices of other goods and services increased even faster, clothing
became cheaper relative to other commodities. At the same time,

TABLE 2   Inflation Adjustments between 1972–1973 and 1981 for Specific Categories of Consumption

| Category of Consumption | Consumer Price Index (1967 = 100) | | Ratio of June 1981 CPI to December 1972 CPI |
|---|---|---|---|
| | December 1972[a] | June 1981 | |
| Food at home | 124.1 | 268.7 | 2.165 |
| Food away from home | 133.7 | 290.6 | 2.174 |
| Shelter | 136.8 | 312.6 | 2.285 |
| Fuel and utilities | 121.9 | 320.2 | 2.627 |
| Household furnishings | 119.5 | 221.1 | 1.850 |
| Clothing | 125.0 | 185.8 | 1.486 |
| Transportation | 121.3 | 279.9 | 2.308 |
| Medical care | 134.4 | 291.5 | 2.169 |
| Entertainment[b] | 127.5 | 220.8 | 1.732 |
| Other goods and services[c] | 129.2 | 233.4 | 1.807 |

SOURCE: U.S. Department of Labor, Bureau of Labor Statistics, Consumer Price Index,
Microfiche Files, August 27, 1981.
a. December 1972 was used as the midpoint of the 1972–1973 period.
b. Price increases for entertainment were applied to our recreation category.
c. "Other goods and services" are used in lieu of a miscellaneous category.

economic theory leads us to expect that a decline in the relative price of clothing would lead to increased consumption of clothing. Similarly, increases in the relative prices of fuel and utilities and of transportation would cause a substitution away from these comparatively higher-priced items in families' budgets. Because we have used data from a single point in time, we have not been able to incorporate fully the effects of changing relative commodity prices on patterns of families' expenditures. We have necessarily assumed that expenditure patterns do not change between 1972–1973 and 1981, and that only relative prices do. As a result, our estimates of child-related expenditures, when disaggregated into separate item-specific categories of consumption, may overstate the importance of commodities whose price increase exceeded the average increase in the overall CPI. The estimates may attribute too little importance to such items as clothing whose price increased less than the national average between 1972–1973 and 1981.

The remainder of this chapter is divided into six major sections. First, we describe our results for the total United States, focusing on variations in parental expenditures connected with differences in the number and ages of children, parents' socioeconomic status, and mothers' employment status. This section will also present new data on the costs of a college education. Following that, we examine results for the major population subgroups (by race, region, and place of residence). Findings on the disaggregation of expenditures on children into the major categories of consumption are presented next, followed by a discussion of the import of variations in both the timing and spacing of children. We then summarize a comparison of our major results from the 1972–1973 Consumer Expenditure Survey (CES) with those from the earlier 1960–1961 BLS Survey of Consumer Expenditures (SCE). Finally, we consider how much a family is likely to spend on rearing a child born in 1981 up to the age of 18. Here we consider future inflation in the United States and present estimates based on three different inflation scenarios.

For the most part, our estimates in this chapter assume that mothers are 25 years old when they have their first child, that births are spaced two years apart, and that husbands are two years older than their wives. Exceptions to this generalization occur when we examine the impact of spacing and timing ot oirths on parental expenditures.

## Estimates for the Total United States

Table 3 presents estimates of parental expenditures on children for the total U.S. population, broken down by level of family income, family

TABLE 3 Parental Expenditures on Children, Total United States, 1981 Prices
(Expenditures in thousands of dollars)

| | | | Wife's Employment Status: Full-time, Full-year Worker | | | | | | | |
| | One-child Families | Two-child Families | | | Three-child Families | | | |
| Socioeconomic Status Group | Age Group | Total | First Child | Second Child | Total | First Child | Second Child | Third Child | Total |
|---|---|---|---|---|---|---|---|---|---|
| High | 0-17 | $135.7 | $107.6 | $102.7 | $210.3 | $93.5 | $86.1 | $83.1 | $262.7 |
| | 0-5 | 35.6 | 31.6 | 23.9 | 55.5 | 32.0 | 22.4 | 16.0 | 70.4 |
| | 6-11 | 49.3 | 37.1 | 38.2 | 75.4 | 30.2 | 30.7 | 31.9 | 92.8 |
| | 12-17 | 50.8 | 38.9 | 40.5 | 79.4 | 31.3 | 33.0 | 35.2 | 99.4 |
| Medium | 0-17 | 121.6 | 96.9 | 91.3 | 188.2 | 84.6 | 76.8 | 73.5 | 234.9 |
| | 0-5 | 32.4 | 29.0 | 21.1 | 50.1 | 29.5 | 20.0 | 13.7 | 63.1 |
| | 6-11 | 44.4 | 33.4 | 34.2 | 67.7 | 27.3 | 27.5 | 28.5 | 83.2 |
| | 12-17 | 44.9 | 34.5 | 36.0 | 70.5 | 27.8 | 29.4 | 31.4 | 88.6 |
| Low | 0-17 | 114.7 | 91.6 | 85.9 | 177.5 | 80.1 | 72.4 | 69.1 | 221.6 |
| | 0-5 | 30.6 | 27.5 | 19.7 | 47.2 | 28.0 | 18.7 | 12.5 | 59.2 |
| | 6-11 | 41.9 | 31.6 | 32.3 | 63.9 | 25.8 | 26.0 | 26.9 | 78.7 |
| | 12-17 | 42.2 | 32.5 | 33.9 | 66.4 | 26.2 | 27.7 | 29.7 | 83.7 |

TABLE 3 Parental Expenditures on Children, Total United States, 1981 Prices
(continued) (*Expenditures in thousands of dollars*)

| Socioeconomic Status Group | Age Group | One-child Families | Wife's Employment Status: Part-time, Full-year Worker | | | | | | |
|---|---|---|---|---|---|---|---|---|---|
| | | | Two-child Families | | | Three-child Families | | | |
| | | Total | First Child | Second Child | Total | First Child | Second Child | Third Child | Total |
| High | 0-17 | $126.3 | $100.2 | $96.4 | $196.6 | $87.1 | $80.8 | $78.6 | $246.4 |
| | 0-5 | 31.6 | 28.3 | 21.3 | 49.5 | 28.7 | 20.0 | 14.2 | 63.0 |
| | 6-11 | 46.1 | 34.8 | 36.1 | 70.9 | 28.3 | 29.0 | 30.3 | 87.7 |
| | 12-17 | 48.6 | 37.2 | 39.0 | 76.2 | 30.0 | 31.7 | 34.0 | 95.7 |
| Medium | 0-17 | 106.2 | 84.9 | 80.0 | 164.8 | 74.3 | 67.4 | 64.7 | 206.4 |
| | 0-5 | 27.4 | 24.7 | 17.5 | 42.2 | 25.4 | 16.7 | 11.0 | 53.1 |
| | 6-11 | 39.0 | 29.4 | 30.3 | 59.7 | 24.1 | 24.4 | 25.3 | 73.8 |
| | 12-17 | 39.8 | 30.7 | 32.2 | 62.9 | 24.8 | 26.3 | 28.4 | 79.6 |
| Low | 0-17 | 96.6 | 77.5 | 72.5 | 149.9 | 68.0 | 61.3 | 58.6 | 187.9 |
| | 0-5 | 24.9 | 22.6 | 15.5 | 38.2 | 23.4 | 15.0 | 9.4 | 47.7 |
| | 6-11 | 35.6 | 26.9 | 27.6 | 54.5 | 22.0 | 22.2 | 23.1 | 67.4 |
| | 12-17 | 36.1 | 27.9 | 29.3 | 57.2 | 22.6 | 24.1 | 26.1 | 72.8 |

TABLE 3    Parental Expenditures on Children, Total United States, 1981 Prices
(continued)    (Expenditures in thousands of dollars)

| Socioeconomic Status Group | Age Group | One-child Families | Wife's Employment Status: Not Employed | | | | | | |
|---|---|---|---|---|---|---|---|---|---|
| | | | Two-child Families | | | Three-child Families | | | |
| | | Total | First Child | Second Child | Total | First Child | Second Child | Third Child | Total |
| High | 0–17 | $117.8 | $93.5 | $90.5 | $184.0 | $81.3 | $75.9 | $74.2 | $231.4 |
| | 0–5 | 28.4 | 25.5 | 19.0 | 44.5 | 26.1 | 18.0 | 12.6 | 56.8 |
| | 6–11 | 43.2 | 32.6 | 34.1 | 66.7 | 26.6 | 27.4 | 28.8 | 82.8 |
| | 12–17 | 46.2 | 35.5 | 37.5 | 72.8 | 28.6 | 30.5 | 32.7 | 91.8 |
| Medium | 0–17 | 98.3 | 78.7 | 74.0 | 152.8 | 69.0 | 62.6 | 60.0 | 191.6 |
| | 0–5 | 24.9 | 22.7 | 15.7 | 38.4 | 23.4 | 15.1 | 9.7 | 48.2 |
| | 6–11 | 36.3 | 27.4 | 28.3 | 55.7 | 22.4 | 22.7 | 23.7 | 68.9 |
| | 12–17 | 37.1 | 28.7 | 30.1 | 58.7 | 23.2 | 24.7 | 26.7 | 74.6 |
| Low | 0–17 | 89.5 | 72.0 | 67.3 | 139.2 | 63.3 | 57.0 | 54.6 | 174.9 |
| | 0–5 | 22.7 | 20.8 | 14.0 | 34.7 | 21.6 | 13.5 | 8.3 | 43.4 |
| | 6–11 | 33.2 | 25.1 | 25.8 | 50.9 | 20.5 | 20.8 | 21.7 | 63.0 |
| | 12–17 | 33.6 | 26.1 | 27.5 | 53.6 | 21.2 | 22.7 | 24.6 | 68.5 |

size, child's birth order, age of child, and wife's employment status. In the following pages, we describe the major differences in estimated expenditures linked with variations in these characteristics.

## Family Income

To highlight the variations in expenditures dependent on level of family income, we have subdivided the families in our sample into three socioeconomic status classifications: high, medium, and low. To reiterate, families are assumed to fall into the high SES group if the husband has a white-collar occupation and some college education. Husbands with a blue-collar job and a high school degree define the medium SES group. And if the husband has a blue-collar job and less than a high school education, the family falls into the low SES category. As one might expect, the estimates indicate that families at the higher socioeconomic levels spend more on their children than those at the lower levels. Consider, for example, a two-child family in which the wife works part time. Table 3 shows that such a family in the high SES group spends an average of $98,300 to raise a child to age 18, while the corresponding estimates for the medium and low SES groups are $82,400 and $74,950, respectively. This same pattern is apparent regardless of the size of the family or the wife's employment status. Put simply, families with larger incomes can be expected to allocate larger sums for their children's upbringing.

## Family Size

First, and most obvious, the figures in table 3 indicate that families with the greatest number of children spend the greatest total amount on child-related purchases. For a three-child family at the medium SES level, where the wife works part time, the total expenditures devoted to children are estimated at $206,400. Expenses for a two-child family are less at $164,800, while a one-child family's total is even lower at $106,200. However, if attention is focused on individual children within families, it becomes clear that expenditures per child decrease as family size grows. For example, consider again the medium-income family where the wife works part time. Our estimates indicate that a family with these characteristics and only one child spends a total of $106,200 on child-related purchases. The same family with two children will spend an average of $82,400 per child, while the three-child family's expenditures per child fall to $68,800. In other words, the larger the family the less the total funds devoted to any individual child, which remains true regardless of the SES status of the family or the employment status of the wife.

## Birth Order

Past research on the expenditures associated with childrearing has shown that the total amount spent raising a child varies with the birth order of the child (Espenshade 1973). Our estimates substantiate this finding. Data from table 3 show that the expenses of rearing an additional child are generally less than those for the preceding child. For example, let us return again to the medium SES two-child family where the wife works part time. Our results indicate that the parents are likely to spend $84,900 on the first child and $80,000 on the second child. This same pattern reappears when we examine the figures for the comparable three-child family. Expenditures for the first child total $74,300, for the second $67,400, and for the third $64,700. These estimates reflect the notion that certain economies of scale are associated with raising children. With the arrival of a first child, parents must often make substantial purchases and investments to accommodate the new addition to their family. Many of these capital outlays need not be repeated for additional children so that in terms of overall expenditures, higher birth order children are somewhat less expensive.

## Age of Child

Total expenditures per child have been allocated among three age intervals: 0-5, 6-11, and 12-17. Distribution of expenditures across these age groups varies somewhat depending on family income level, family size, birth order of child, and employment status of the wife. However, some generalizations can be made. Overall, approximately 26 percent of the total expenditures are incurred between the time the child is born and the time he or she reaches age 6. The remaining expenses are divided almost evenly between the other two age groups—roughly 36 percent of the remainder is allocated to the 6-11 age interval and 38 percent to the 12-17 age group. In other words, nearly 75 percent of the total expenditures occur when the child is between age 6 and 17. For example, let us examine the data for our two-child, medium SES family where the wife works part time. Total expenditures for an average child would be approximately $82,400. Of this total, the breakdown is as follows: 25.6 percent of the total is spent when the child is in the 0-5 age group, 36.2 percent when the child is 6-11, and 38.2 percent when the child is 12-17. These findings are what we would expect since it is generally agreed that the greatest expenses of childrearing occur when the child is a teenager.

Our findings indicate that expenses are distributed by age somewhat differently for higher birth order children than for firstborns. Expenditures made for the second and third child when they are in the 0-5 age group generally comprise a smaller proportion of the child's total budget than similar expenditures do for eldest children. For example, in a medium SES two-child family where the wife works part time, 21.9 percent of the expenses for the second child are incurred before the child reaches age 6. The comparable figure for the first child in the same family is 29.1 percent. Expenditures on the second child at ages 6-11 make up 37.9 percent of the total and 40.3 percent at ages 12-17. For the first child, the comparable estimates are 34.6 percent and 36.2 percent, respectively. Economies of scale associated with raising more than one child concentrate in the children's earlier years.

## Employment Status of Wife

The employment status of the wife is included in our breakdown of family characteristics for information on the possible impacts of a mother's contribution to family income. As mentioned earlier, we chose three possible scenarios regarding the wife's employment status—wife employed full time, full year; wife employed part time, full year; and wife not employed. The pattern of the expenditure estimates across the various employment statuses of the wife are much as one would expect. Families in which the wife works full time spend more on their children than do those in which the wife works only part time or not at all. For example, a medium SES family with two children spends approximately $94,100 per child if the wife is employed full time. If the wife works only part time, the estimate falls to $82,400 and to $76,400 if the wife does not work at all. The funds contributed by the working mother to the family income noticeably affect the total amount of money spent on rearing children.

## College Costs

The estimates of parental expenditures on children presented in table 3 do not include any allowances for the potential cost of a college education. Because this is important in estimating the total expenditures many parents can expect to face, we include some recent data on the costs of postsecondary education.

Table 4 itemizes the one-year costs of matriculation at both public and private colleges for resident students in the 1981–1982 academic year. According to these figures, calculated by the College Board, total expenses range from a low of $3,230 for a public two-year college to a high of $6,885 for a private four-year institution. Generally, the greatest portion of the college bill goes to pay for room and board at a public college and for tuition and fees at a private college. To arrive at an estimate of total college expenses, simply multiply the yearly cost at the chosen type of institution by the expected years in attendance. For example, if the child expects to graduate from a four-year public college, the total cost will be approximately $15,492 ($3,873 per year × 4 years).

## Total Expenditures from Birth to College

An estimate of the total expenditures parents can expect to make to raise their child from birth through college can be derived by combining the total direct costs shown in table 3 with the total college costs from table 4. Table 5 summarizes these costs for each of the three socioeconomic status groups. Figures are presented for an average child in a two-child family where the wife is assumed to work part time. For the purposes of illustration we assumed that the child from the high SES family would spend four years at a private college, the medium SES child would attend a four-year public college, and the low SES child would go to a two-year public college. These choices are somewhat arbitrary. No hard and fast rule states that a child from a high SES family will attend a private college for four years; many study at two-year public colleges, and some end their formal schooling after high school.

TABLE 4    Average Annual Expenses for Resident Students at Private and Public Colleges, 1981–1982 Academic Year

|  | Two-year Institutions | | Four-year Institutions | |
|---|---|---|---|---|
| Item | Public | Private | Public | Private |
| Tuition and fees | $   469 | $2,632 | $   819 | $3,709 |
| Books and supplies | 235 | 241 | 251 | 263 |
| Room and board | 1,615 | 1,926 | 1,846 | 2,043 |
| Personal expenses | 583 | 529 | 667 | 557 |
| Transportation | 328 | 276 | 290 | 313 |
| Total expenses | $3,230 | $5,604 | $3,873 | $6,885 |

SOURCE: College Entrance Examination Board. *The College Cost Book, 1981–82.* Second Edition. New York, 1981.

TABLE 5   Estimated Total Parental Expenditures for an Average Child (in a
Two-child Family, Assuming the Wife Works Part Time, 1981 Prices)

| *Socioeconomic Status Group* | *Direct Expenditures from Birth to Age 18* | *College Costs* | *Combined Total* |
|---|---|---|---|
| High SES | $98,300 | $27,540[a] | $125,840 |
| Medium SES | 82,400 | 15,492[b] | 97,892 |
| Low SES | 74,950 | 6,460[c] | 81,410 |

a. Assumes the child will attend a four-year private college.
b. Assumes the child will attend a four-year public college.
c. Assumes the child will attend a two-year public college.

Estimates shown in table 5 disclose that total expenditures can range from a low of $81,410 for the low SES child attending a two-year public college to a high of $125,840 for the high SES child who spends four years at a private college. Variations in the actual amount spent are likely, depending on the choices made about the type of educational institution attended.

## Results for Population Subgroups

Besides the estimates of parental expenditures on children for the total U.S. population, we prepared similar estimates for several major subgroups of the population. We were interested chiefly in differences associated with race, region of the country, and place of residence. We considered two racial groups (white and other than black, and black), four census regions (Northeast, North Central, South, and West), and two residential locations (inside SMSAs and outside SMSAs). Table 6 shows the distribution of our sample of husband-wife households along each of these dimensions.

To produce estimates of child-related expenditures separately for black and white families, the total sample was divided into two parts. The regression specifications used for the total U.S. sample for husband's earnings, wife's earnings, total family consumption, consumption patterns, and the standard-of-living (SOL) equation were reestimated separately on the black and white subsamples.[1] Estimates for the four census regions and by metropolitan status were produced in the same manner, by first dividing the total sample either by region or by place of residence and then reestimating the total U.S. specifications on each subsample. Consequently, we do not generate estimates for cases where race, region, and

TABLE 6   Distribution of Total Sample, 1972-1973

| Race of Head of Consumer Unit | | |
| --- | --- | --- |
| Category | Number | Percentage |
| White and other than black | 7,959 | 93.1 |
| Black | 588 | 6.9 |
| Total | 8,547 | 100.0 |

| Census Region | | |
| --- | --- | --- |
| Category | Number | Percentage |
| Northeast | 1,788 | 20.9 |
| North Central | 2,452 | 28.7 |
| South | 2,536 | 29.7 |
| West | 1,771 | 20.7 |
| Total | 8,547 | 100.0 |

| Place of Residence | | |
| --- | --- | --- |
| Category | Number | Percentage |
| Metropolitan (inside SMSAs) | 6,038 | 70.6 |
| Nonmetropolitan (outside SMSAs) | 2,509 | 29.4 |
| Total | 8,547 | 100.0 |

residence are considered jointly. That is, we do not have estimates, for example, for black families living in metropolitan areas in the Northeast. The following sections describe the main differences in child-related expenditures within the various subgroups of race, region, and residence.

## Race

Tables 7 and 8 present estimates of parental expenditures computed separately for white and black families. For the sake of simplicity, we include data for only two of the three possible employment statuses of the wife—wife assumed to work full time, full year and wife assumed to have zero earnings. These findings demonstrate that white families generally spend more on their children than do comparable black families, although the differences are not striking. Figures from tables 7 and 8 reveal that a white family at the medium SES level with two children and a wife who works full time spends an average of $93,850 to raise a child from birth to age 18. A similar black family's total expenditures for that

TABLE 7 Parental Expenditures on Children by Race of Head and Employment Status of Wife, in 1981 Prices (Expenditures in thousands of dollars)

| Socioeconomic Status Group | Age Group | One-child Families | | | Wife's Employment Status: Full-time, Full-year Worker Two-child Families | | | | | | | | |
| | | Total United States Total | Total Whites Total | Total Blacks Total | Total United States First Child | Second Child | Total | Whites First Child | Second Child | Total | Blacks First Child | Second Child | Total |
|---|---|---|---|---|---|---|---|---|---|---|---|---|---|
| High | 0–17 | $135.7 | $143.2 | $124.7 | $107.6 | $102.7 | $210.3 | $113.6 | $109.0 | $222.6 | $96.4 | $94.1 | $190.5 |
| | 0–5 | 35.6 | 36.4 | 37.6 | 31.6 | 23.9 | 55.5 | 32.5 | 24.9 | 57.3 | 31.7 | 27.5 | 59.2 |
| | 6–11 | 49.3 | 51.7 | 45.0 | 37.1 | 38.2 | 75.4 | 38.9 | 40.1 | 78.9 | 33.8 | 33.3 | 67.1 |
| | 12–17 | 50.8 | 55.1 | 42.1 | 38.9 | 40.5 | 79.4 | 42.3 | 44.0 | 86.3 | 30.9 | 33.3 | 64.2 |
| Medium | 0–17 | 121.6 | 121.2 | 118.6 | 96.9 | 91.3 | 188.2 | 96.9 | 90.8 | 187.7 | 91.6 | 90.4 | 182.0 |
| | 0–5 | 32.4 | 32.1 | 34.8 | 29.0 | 21.1 | 50.1 | 28.9 | 20.9 | 49.8 | 29.4 | 25.5 | 54.9 |
| | 6–11 | 44.4 | 44.0 | 42.6 | 33.4 | 34.2 | 67.7 | 33.1 | 33.7 | 66.8 | 32.0 | 31.8 | 63.8 |
| | 12–17 | 44.9 | 45.2 | 41.2 | 34.5 | 36.0 | 70.5 | 34.9 | 36.2 | 71.1 | 30.2 | 33.0 | 63.2 |
| Low | 0–17 | 114.7 | 112.4 | 110.8 | 91.6 | 85.9 | 177.5 | 90.2 | 84.0 | 174.2 | 85.7 | 84.2 | 169.8 |
| | 0–5 | 30.6 | 29.8 | 32.8 | 27.5 | 19.7 | 47.2 | 27.0 | 19.1 | 46.0 | 27.7 | 23.9 | 51.6 |
| | 6–11 | 41.9 | 40.8 | 39.9 | 31.6 | 32.3 | 63.9 | 30.8 | 31.3 | 62.1 | 30.0 | 29.7 | 59.7 |
| | 12–17 | 42.2 | 41.8 | 38.1 | 32.5 | 33.9 | 66.4 | 32.4 | 33.6 | 66.0 | 27.9 | 30.5 | 58.5 |

TABLE 7 Parental Expenditures on Children by Race of Head and Employment Status of Wife, in 1981 Prices
(continued) (Expenditures in thousands of dollars)

*Wife's Employment Status: Full-time, Full-year Worker, Three-child Families*

| Socioeconomic Status Group | Age Group | Total United States | | | | Whites | | | | Blacks | | | |
|---|---|---|---|---|---|---|---|---|---|---|---|---|---|
| | | First Child | Second Child | Third Child | Total | First Child | Second Child | Third Child | Total | First Child | Second Child | Third Child | Total |
| High | 0–17 | $93.5 | $86.1 | $83.1 | $262.7 | $98.8 | $91.5 | $88.4 | $278.8 | $81.9 | $76.7 | $76.6 | $235.2 |
| | 0–5 | 32.0 | 22.4 | 16.0 | 70.4 | 32.9 | 23.4 | 17.0 | 73.3 | 30.3 | 24.0 | 21.0 | 75.3 |
| | 6–11 | 30.2 | 30.7 | 31.9 | 92.8 | 31.5 | 32.2 | 33.3 | 97.1 | 27.7 | 26.7 | 26.7 | 81.1 |
| | 12–17 | 31.3 | 33.0 | 35.2 | 99.4 | 34.4 | 36.0 | 38.1 | 108.4 | 23.9 | 26.0 | 28.9 | 78.8 |
| Medium | 0–17 | 84.6 | 76.8 | 73.5 | 234.9 | 85.0 | 76.8 | 72.8 | 234.6 | 77.7 | 73.6 | 74.4 | 225.6 |
| | 0–5 | 29.5 | 20.0 | 13.7 | 63.1 | 29.5 | 19.9 | 13.4 | 62.9 | 28.0 | 22.3 | 19.7 | 70.0 |
| | 6–11 | 27.3 | 27.5 | 28.5 | 83.2 | 27.0 | 27.1 | 27.8 | 81.9 | 26.3 | 25.6 | 25.8 | 77.6 |
| | 12–17 | 27.8 | 29.4 | 31.4 | 88.6 | 28.5 | 29.7 | 31.5 | 89.8 | 23.3 | 25.8 | 28.9 | 78.0 |
| Low | 0–17 | 80.1 | 72.4 | 69.1 | 221.6 | 79.3 | 71.2 | 67.3 | 217.8 | 72.7 | 68.6 | 69.1 | 210.4 |
| | 0–5 | 28.0 | 18.7 | 12.5 | 59.2 | 27.7 | 18.2 | 11.9 | 57.9 | 26.4 | 20.9 | 18.3 | 65.7 |
| | 6–11 | 25.8 | 26.0 | 26.9 | 78.7 | 25.1 | 25.2 | 25.9 | 76.2 | 24.7 | 23.9 | 24.0 | 72.5 |
| | 12–17 | 26.2 | 27.7 | 29.7 | 83.7 | 26.5 | 27.7 | 29.5 | 83.8 | 21.5 | 23.8 | 26.8 | 72.2 |

TABLE 8 Parental Expenditures on Children by Race of Head and Employment Status of Wife, in 1981 Prices
(Expenditures in thousands of dollars)

| | | One-child Families | | | Wife's Employment Status: Not Employed — Two-child Families | | | | | | | | |
| | | Total United States | Total Whites | Total Blacks | Total United States | | | Whites | | | Blacks | | |
| Socioeconomic Status Group | Age Group | Total | Total | Total | First Child | Second Child | Total | First Child | Second Child | Total | First Child | Second Child | Total |
|---|---|---|---|---|---|---|---|---|---|---|---|---|---|
| High | 0-17 | $117.8 | $117.3 | $125.5 | $93.5 | $90.5 | $184.0 | $93.5 | $89.7 | $183.2 | $96.0 | $100.7 | $196.7 |
| | 0-5 | 28.4 | 28.3 | 29.9 | 25.5 | 19.0 | 44.5 | 25.6 | 18.9 | 44.5 | 25.0 | 24.1 | 49.1 |
| | 6-11 | 43.2 | 42.7 | 45.5 | 32.6 | 34.1 | 66.7 | 32.2 | 33.4 | 65.6 | 34.1 | 35.8 | 70.0 |
| | 12-17 | 46.2 | 46.2 | 50.2 | 35.5 | 37.4 | 72.8 | 35.7 | 37.4 | 73.1 | 36.9 | 40.7 | 77.6 |
| Medium | 0-17 | 98.3 | 98.1 | 82.6 | 78.7 | 74.0 | 152.8 | 79.0 | 73.6 | 152.6 | 63.9 | 63.2 | 127.0 |
| | 0-5 | 24.9 | 25.1 | 23.9 | 22.7 | 15.7 | 38.4 | 22.9 | 15.7 | 38.6 | 20.2 | 17.5 | 37.7 |
| | 6-11 | 36.3 | 35.9 | 30.1 | 27.4 | 28.3 | 55.7 | 27.1 | 27.7 | 54.9 | 22.8 | 22.4 | 45.1 |
| | 12-17 | 37.1 | 37.1 | 28.6 | 28.7 | 30.1 | 58.7 | 28.9 | 30.1 | 59.0 | 20.9 | 23.3 | 44.2 |
| Low | 0-17 | 89.5 | 89.8 | 82.6 | 72.0 | 67.3 | 139.2 | 72.6 | 67.2 | 139.8 | 63.9 | 63.2 | 127.0 |
| | 0-5 | 22.7 | 22.9 | 23.9 | 20.8 | 14.0 | 34.7 | 21.1 | 14.0 | 35.1 | 20.2 | 17.5 | 37.7 |
| | 6-11 | 33.2 | 33.0 | 30.1 | 25.1 | 25.8 | 50.9 | 24.9 | 25.4 | 50.4 | 22.8 | 22.4 | 45.1 |
| | 12-17 | 33.6 | 33.9 | 28.6 | 26.1 | 27.5 | 53.6 | 26.6 | 27.7 | 54.3 | 20.9 | 23.3 | 44.2 |

TABLE 8   Parental Expenditures on Children by Race of Head and Employment Status of Wife, in 1981 Prices
(continued)   (Expenditures in thousands of dollars)

Wife's Employment Status: Not Employed. Three-child Families

| Socioeconomic Status Group | Age Group | Total United States | | | | Whites | | | | Blacks | | | |
|---|---|---|---|---|---|---|---|---|---|---|---|---|---|
| | | First Child | Second Child | Third Child | Total | First Child | Second Child | Third Child | Total | First Child | Second Child | Third Child | Total |
| High | 0–17 | $81.3 | $75.9 | $74.2 | $231.4 | $81.7 | $75.6 | $73.2 | $230.6 | $80.2 | $81.5 | $86.0 | $247.7 |
| | 0–5 | 26.1 | 18.0 | 12.6 | 56.8 | 26.4 | 18.0 | 12.4 | 56.9 | 23.7 | 20.9 | 20.1 | 64.7 |
| | 6–11 | 26.6 | 27.4 | 28.8 | 82.8 | 26.2 | 26.9 | 28.1 | 81.2 | 28.0 | 28.7 | 30.3 | 87.0 |
| | 12–17 | 28.6 | 30.5 | 32.7 | 91.8 | 29.1 | 30.7 | 32.8 | 92.5 | 28.6 | 31.8 | 35.7 | 96.1 |
| Medium | 0–17 | 69.0 | 62.6 | 60.0 | 191.6 | 69.7 | 62.5 | 59.3 | 191.5 | 54.1 | 51.4 | 52.4 | 158.0 |
| | 0–5 | 23.4 | 15.1 | 9.7 | 48.2 | 23.8 | 15.2 | 9.5 | 48.5 | 19.2 | 15.3 | 13.4 | 47.8 |
| | 6–11 | 22.4 | 22.7 | 23.7 | 68.9 | 22.2 | 22.4 | 23.1 | 67.6 | 18.9 | 18.0 | 18.1 | 55.0 |
| | 12–17 | 23.2 | 24.7 | 26.7 | 74.6 | 23.7 | 24.9 | 26.7 | 75.4 | 16.1 | 18.1 | 21.0 | 55.2 |
| Low | 0–17 | 63.3 | 57.0 | 54.6 | 174.9 | 64.3 | 57.3 | 54.2 | 175.8 | 54.1 | 51.4 | 52.4 | 158.0 |
| | 0–5 | 21.6 | 13.5 | 8.3 | 43.4 | 22.0 | 13.7 | 8.2 | 43.9 | 19.2 | 15.3 | 13.4 | 47.8 |
| | 6–11 | 20.5 | 20.8 | 21.7 | 63.0 | 20.4 | 20.5 | 21.2 | 62.1 | 18.9 | 18.0 | 18.1 | 55.0 |
| | 12–17 | 21.2 | 22.7 | 24.6 | 68.5 | 21.9 | 23.1 | 24.8 | 69.8 | 16.1 | 18.1 | 21.0 | 55.2 |

same child are estimated at $91,000. An exception to this pattern is high SES families in which the wife does not work. Regardless of the size of the family, black families in that category spend more on child-related purchases than do comparable white families. A high-income level black family with two children and a nonworking wife spends $98,350 per child while the same white family spends an average of $91,600 per child.

This atypical finding may reflect actual black-white differences in behavior among high SES families in which the wife does not work. But it may also be because of a disproportionately small number of high SES black families in our sample. Table 9 presents a breakdown by race of the number of families in each socioeconomic status group. There are only 49 black families in the high SES group compared with 1,899 white families in the same category. This small sample size has some effect on our estimates.

## Region

Estimates were computed separately for each of the four U.S. census regions—Northeast, North Central, South, and West. Tables 10 and 11 present these figures for families in which the wife is employed full time and those in which the wife is assumed to have zero earnings.

Detecting any consistent pattern regarding regional variations in child-related expenditures is difficult. Generally, parents in the Northeast and the West devote larger sums to their children's upbringing than do parents in the North Central and South regions. However, this conclusion is sensitive to variations in the size of the family, the level of family income, and the employment status of the wife. If we focus only on those families in which the wife stays at home (table 11), more definite patterns emerge. The total expenditures on children in these families are consistently highest for those residing in the West and lowest for those in the South, regardless of other family characteristics. Returning again to the

TABLE 9   Number of Black and White Families in Sample

| Socioeconomic Status Group | White Families | | Black Families | |
|---|---|---|---|---|
| | Number | Percentage | Number | Percentage |
| High | 1,899 | 35.2 | 49 | 11.3 |
| Medium | 1,942 | 36.0 | 156 | 36.1 |
| Low | 1,552 | 28.8 | 227 | 52.5 |
| Total | 5,393 | 100.0 | 432 | 100.0 |

TABLE 10    Parental Expenditures on Children by Census Region and Employment Status of Wife, in 1981 Prices
(*Expenditures in thousands of dollars*)

| Socioeconomic Status Group | Age Group | Wife's Employment Status: Full-time, Full-year Worker, One-child Families | | | | |
|---|---|---|---|---|---|---|
| | | Total United States Total | Northeast Total | North Central Total | South Total | West Total |
| High | 0–17 | $135.7 | $158.7 | $133.4 | $144.7 | $146.6 |
| | 0–5 | 35.6 | 41.3 | 35.4 | 36.3 | 40.0 |
| | 6–11 | 49.3 | 56.6 | 48.5 | 52.7 | 51.9 |
| | 12–17 | 50.8 | 60.8 | 49.5 | 55.6 | 54.7 |
| Medium | 0–17 | 121.6 | 125.5 | 125.5 | 110.7 | 135.1 |
| | 0–5 | 32.4 | 34.8 | 33.1 | 29.5 | 37.5 |
| | 6–11 | 44.4 | 45.1 | 45.7 | 40.8 | 47.8 |
| | 12–17 | 44.9 | 45.6 | 46.7 | 40.4 | 49.8 |
| Low | 0–17 | 114.7 | 118.3 | 121.6 | 97.6 | 129.4 |
| | 0–5 | 30.6 | 33.1 | 32.1 | 26.1 | 36.0 |
| | 6–11 | 41.9 | 42.5 | 44.3 | 36.0 | 45.8 |
| | 12–17 | 42.2 | 42.7 | 45.2 | 35.5 | 47.6 |

two-child family at the medium-income level, we find that a family in the
West spends an average of $90,650 per child compared with an estimated
$65,000 for the same-status child in a family in the South.

## Place of Residence

Tables 12 and 13 present estimates for child-related expenditures by
family place of residence, defined here as metropolitan (inside SMSAs) or
nonmetropolitan (outside SMSAs). As in the previous sets of tables,
results are displayed for only two of the possible situations regarding the
wife's employment. The figures in tables 12 and 13 indicate a marked difference in the total amount of funds devoted to childrearing by families in
the two types of residences. Families in metropolitan areas consistently
spend more on their children, regardless of family size or wife's employment status. Our estimates show that a two-child family at the medium-
income level with a wife employed full time spends $98,700 rearing a child
to age 18 if the family resides in a metropolitan area and only $83,500 if
the family lives in a nonmetropolitan area.

TABLE 10 Parental Expenditures on Children by Census Region and Employment Status of Wife, in 1981 Prices
*(continued)* *(Expenditures in thousands of dollars)*

Wife's Employment Status: Full-time, Full-year Worker, Two-child Families

| Socioeconomic Status Group | Age Group | Total United States | | | Northeast | | | North Central | | | South | | | West | | |
|---|---|---|---|---|---|---|---|---|---|---|---|---|---|---|---|---|
| | | First Child | Second Child | Total | First Child | Second Child | Total | First Child | Second Child | Total | First Child | Second Child | Total | First Child | Second Child | Total |
| High | 0–17 | $107.6 | $102.7 | $210.3 | $125.1 | $124.5 | $249.6 | $106.4 | $101.1 | $207.5 | $114.0 | $107.9 | $221.9 | $115.7 | $114.4 | $230.1 |
| | 0–5 | 31.6 | 23.9 | 55.5 | 36.8 | 30.7 | 67.5 | 31.6 | 23.7 | 55.3 | 31.6 | 24.6 | 56.2 | 34.1 | 30.3 | 64.4 |
| | 6–11 | 37.1 | 38.2 | 75.4 | 41.5 | 44.1 | 85.6 | 36.3 | 37.8 | 74.1 | 40.4 | 40.2 | 80.5 | 39.4 | 41.0 | 80.3 |
| | 12–17 | 38.9 | 40.5 | 79.4 | 46.8 | 49.6 | 96.4 | 38.5 | 39.6 | 78.1 | 42.0 | 43.2 | 85.2 | 42.2 | 43.1 | 85.3 |
| Medium | 0–17 | 96.9 | 91.3 | 188.2 | 99.6 | 96.8 | 196.3 | 100.3 | 95.1 | 195.4 | 88.3 | 80.2 | 168.5 | 106.8 | 105.1 | 211.9 |
| | 0–5 | 29.0 | 21.1 | 50.1 | 31.2 | 24.9 | 56.1 | 29.7 | 21.9 | 51.6 | 26.0 | 18.6 | 44.6 | 32.1 | 28.1 | 60.1 |
| | 6–11 | 33.4 | 34.2 | 67.7 | 33.0 | 34.5 | 67.5 | 34.2 | 35.6 | 69.8 | 31.4 | 30.3 | 61.7 | 36.2 | 37.6 | 73.9 |
| | 12–17 | 34.5 | 36.0 | 70.5 | 35.4 | 37.4 | 72.7 | 36.4 | 37.5 | 73.9 | 30.9 | 31.4 | 62.2 | 38.5 | 39.4 | 77.9 |
| Low | 0–17 | 91.6 | 85.9 | 177.5 | 94.0 | 91.1 | 185.1 | 97.3 | 92.0 | 189.3 | 78.2 | 70.4 | 148.6 | 102.4 | 100.6 | 203.0 |
| | 0–5 | 27.5 | 19.7 | 47.2 | 29.7 | 23.4 | 53.1 | 28.9 | 21.2 | 50.0 | 23.1 | 15.9 | 39.0 | 30.8 | 26.8 | 57.7 |
| | 6–11 | 31.6 | 32.3 | 63.9 | 31.1 | 32.5 | 63.6 | 33.2 | 34.5 | 67.7 | 27.8 | 26.7 | 54.5 | 34.7 | 36.1 | 70.8 |
| | 12–17 | 32.5 | 33.9 | 66.4 | 33.2 | 35.2 | 68.4 | 35.2 | 36.3 | 71.5 | 27.2 | 27.8 | 55.1 | 36.9 | 37.7 | 74.6 |

TABLE 10  Parental Expenditures on Children by Census Region and Employment Status of Wife, in 1981 Prices
(continued)  (Expenditures in thousands of dollars)

Wife's Employment Status: Full-time, Full-year Worker. Three-child Families

| Socioeconomic Status Group | Age Group | Total United States | | | | Northeast | | | | North Central | | | |
|---|---|---|---|---|---|---|---|---|---|---|---|---|---|
| | | First Child | Second Child | Third Child | Total | First Child | Second Child | Third Child | Total | First Child | Second Child | Third Child | Total |
| High | 0–17 | $93.5 | $86.1 | $83.1 | $262.7 | $107.6 | $103.4 | $105.0 | $316.0 | $92.8 | $85.1 | $81.9 | $259.8 |
| | 0–5 | 32.0 | 22.4 | 16.0 | 70.4 | 37.0 | 28.3 | 23.8 | 89.1 | 31.9 | 22.3 | 16.3 | 70.5 |
| | 6–11 | 30.2 | 30.7 | 31.9 | 92.8 | 32.5 | 34.5 | 37.1 | 104.1 | 29.1 | 30.1 | 31.3 | 90.6 |
| | 12–17 | 31.3 | 33.0 | 35.2 | 99.4 | 38.0 | 40.6 | 44.1 | 122.8 | 31.7 | 32.8 | 34.3 | 98.8 |
| Medium | 0–17 | 84.6 | 76.8 | 73.5 | 234.9 | 86.4 | 80.7 | 80.8 | 247.9 | 87.6 | 80.2 | 77.2 | 245.0 |
| | 0–5 | 29.5 | 20.0 | 13.7 | 63.1 | 31.6 | 23.0 | 18.5 | 73.2 | 30.1 | 20.7 | 14.8 | 65.6 |
| | 6–11 | 27.3 | 27.5 | 28.5 | 83.2 | 25.8 | 26.9 | 28.6 | 81.4 | 27.4 | 28.4 | 29.6 | 85.4 |
| | 12–17 | 27.8 | 29.4 | 31.4 | 88.6 | 28.9 | 30.8 | 33.7 | 93.4 | 30.1 | 31.1 | 32.7 | 93.9 |
| Low | 0–17 | 80.1 | 72.4 | 69.1 | 221.6 | 81.7 | 76.1 | 76.2 | 234.0 | 85.1 | 77.6 | 74.6 | 237.3 |
| | 0–5 | 28.0 | 18.7 | 12.5 | 59.2 | 30.1 | 21.6 | 17.3 | 69.1 | 29.3 | 20.0 | 14.2 | 63.5 |
| | 6–11 | 25.8 | 26.0 | 26.9 | 78.7 | 24.3 | 25.3 | 26.9 | 76.6 | 26.6 | 27.5 | 28.7 | 82.8 |
| | 12–17 | 26.2 | 27.7 | 29.7 | 83.7 | 27.2 | 29.1 | 32.0 | 88.3 | 29.1 | 30.1 | 31.7 | 91.0 |

TABLE 10    Parental Expenditures on Children by Census Region and Employment Status of Wife, in 1981 Prices
(continued)    (Expenditures in thousands of dollars)

*Wife's Employment Status: Full-time, Full-year Worker, Three-child Families*

| Socioeconomic Status Group | Age Group | South | | | | West | | | |
|---|---|---|---|---|---|---|---|---|---|
| | | First Child | Second Child | Third Child | Total | First Child | Second Child | Third Child | Total |
| High | 0–17 | $98.6 | $89.9 | $85.9 | $274.4 | $99.0 | $95.3 | $95.6 | $289.9 |
| | 0–5 | 31.3 | 22.4 | 16.7 | 70.4 | 33.5 | 26.8 | 24.5 | 84.8 |
| | 6–11 | 33.9 | 32.8 | 33.2 | 99.9 | 31.2 | 33.1 | 34.3 | 98.5 |
| | 12–17 | 33.3 | 34.7 | 36.1 | 104.1 | 34.3 | 35.4 | 36.9 | 106.6 |
| Medium | 0–17 | 77.2 | 67.6 | 62.7 | 207.4 | 91.6 | 87.7 | 87.7 | 267.0 |
| | 0–5 | 26.0 | 17.2 | 11.5 | 54.8 | 31.6 | 24.9 | 22.4 | 78.9 |
| | 6–11 | 26.7 | 24.9 | 24.7 | 76.3 | 28.7 | 30.4 | 31.5 | 90.5 |
| | 12–17 | 24.5 | 25.4 | 26.4 | 76.4 | 31.4 | 32.4 | 33.8 | 97.6 |
| Low | 0–17 | 68.6 | 59.5 | 55.1 | 183.2 | 87.8 | 84.0 | 84.1 | 255.9 |
| | 0–5 | 23.2 | 14.9 | 9.5 | 47.6 | 30.3 | 23.9 | 21.4 | 75.6 |
| | 6–11 | 23.7 | 22.0 | 21.8 | 67.5 | 27.4 | 29.1 | 30.2 | 86.7 |
| | 12–17 | 21.7 | 22.7 | 23.7 | 68.1 | 30.0 | 31.0 | 32.5 | 93.6 |

TABLE 11   Parental Expenditures on Children by Census Region and Employment Status of Wife, in 1981 Prices
(*Expenditures in thousands of dollars*)

| | | Wife's Employment Status: Not Employed, One-child Families | | | | |
|---|---|---|---|---|---|---|
| Socioeconomic Status Group | Age Group | Total United States Total | Northeast Total | North Central Total | South Total | West Total |
| High | 0–17 | $117.8 | $127.3 | $119.4 | $111.0 | $128.0 |
| | 0–5 | 28.4 | 32.8 | 28.2 | 26.7 | 33.5 |
| | 6–11 | 43.2 | 45.6 | 43.7 | 41.0 | 45.6 |
| | 12–17 | 46.2 | 48.9 | 47.4 | 43.3 | 49.0 |
| Medium | 0–17 | 98.3 | 102.8 | 103.2 | 85.0 | 115.2 |
| | 0–5 | 24.9 | 28.2 | 25.8 | 22.0 | 31.3 |
| | 6–11 | 36.3 | 37.1 | 38.0 | 31.7 | 40.9 |
| | 12–17 | 37.1 | 37.5 | 39.5 | 31.4 | 43.0 |
| Low | 0–17 | 89.5 | 98.1 | 96.2 | 74.5 | 107.1 |
| | 0–5 | 22.7 | 27.0 | 24.2 | 19.2 | 29.2 |
| | 6–11 | 33.2 | 35.4 | 35.5 | 27.8 | 38.0 |
| | 12–17 | 33.6 | 35.7 | 36.4 | 27.5 | 39.9 |

## Expenditures by Categories of Consumption

To provide information on the distribution of total expenditures
among the various components, estimates were also computed separately
for each of ten major categories of expenditures: food at home; food away
from home; shelter; fuel and utilities; household goods; clothing; transportation; health care; recreation; and miscellaneous. These breakdowns
are presented in tables 14, 15, and 16 for the three family income levels,
for one-, two-, and three-child families, and for the three possible employment statuses of the wife—wife assumed to work full time, full year; wife
assumed to work part time, full year; and wife assumed to have zero
earnings.

Data in these tables reveal that transportation expenses generally
take up the largest portion of the child's budget, followed by expenditures
on food at home. Either fuel and utilities or food away from home appears
to be the least expensive component of total expenditures. For the purposes of illustration consider again the medium SES, two-child family
where the wife is employed part time. Approximately $20,700 per child or
25.1 percent of the total expenditures to age 18 is devoted to transportation expenses. One explanation for the large expense of providing

**TABLE 11** (*continued*)   Parental Expenditures on Children by Census Region and Employment Status of Wife, in 1981 Prices (*Expenditures in thousands of dollars*)

*Wife's Employment Status: Not Employed. Two-child Families*

| Socioeconomic Status Group | Age Group | Total United States | | | Northeast | | | North Central | | | South | | | West | | |
|---|---|---|---|---|---|---|---|---|---|---|---|---|---|---|---|---|
| | | First Child | Second Child | Total | First Child | Second Child | Total | First Child | Second Child | Total | First Child | Second Child | Total | First Child | Second Child | Total |
| High | 0-17 | $93.5 | $90.5 | $184.0 | $100.6 | $100.2 | $200.8 | $95.1 | $92.6 | $187.7 | $88.1 | $82.6 | $170.7 | $101.0 | $101.0 | $202.0 |
| | 0-5 | 25.5 | 19.0 | 44.5 | 29.4 | 24.1 | 53.5 | 25.4 | 19.2 | 44.6 | 23.6 | 17.4 | 41.0 | 28.6 | 25.6 | 54.2 |
| | 6-11 | 32.6 | 34.1 | 66.7 | 33.3 | 35.6 | 69.0 | 32.7 | 34.9 | 67.6 | 31.6 | 31.3 | 62.9 | 34.5 | 36.4 | 70.9 |
| | 12-17 | 35.5 | 37.4 | 72.8 | 37.8 | 40.5 | 78.3 | 37.0 | 38.5 | 75.5 | 33.0 | 33.9 | 66.9 | 37.9 | 38.9 | 76.9 |
| Medium | 0-17 | 78.7 | 74.0 | 152.8 | 81.8 | 79.7 | 161.5 | 82.8 | 78.7 | 161.5 | 68.4 | 61.5 | 130.0 | 91.2 | 90.2 | 181.3 |
| | 0-5 | 22.7 | 15.7 | 38.4 | 25.4 | 19.9 | 45.3 | 23.4 | 16.7 | 40.1 | 19.6 | 13.2 | 32.9 | 26.8 | 23.4 | 50.2 |
| | 6-11 | 27.4 | 28.3 | 55.7 | 27.1 | 28.5 | 55.6 | 28.4 | 30.0 | 58.4 | 24.6 | 23.6 | 48.2 | 31.0 | 32.5 | 63.5 |
| | 12-17 | 28.7 | 30.1 | 58.7 | 29.3 | 31.3 | 60.7 | 31.0 | 32.1 | 63.0 | 24.2 | 24.7 | 49.0 | 33.4 | 34.3 | 67.7 |
| Low | 0-17 | 72.0 | 67.3 | 139.2 | 78.1 | 76.0 | 154.1 | 77.3 | 73.0 | 150.3 | 60.3 | 53.8 | 114.1 | 84.9 | 83.9 | 168.8 |
| | 0-5 | 20.8 | 14.0 | 34.7 | 24.4 | 18.9 | 43.3 | 22.1 | 15.4 | 37.5 | 17.3 | 11.2 | 28.5 | 25.1 | 21.7 | 46.7 |
| | 6-11 | 25.1 | 25.8 | 50.9 | 25.8 | 27.2 | 52.9 | 26.6 | 28.0 | 54.6 | 21.6 | 20.6 | 42.2 | 28.8 | 30.3 | 59.1 |
| | 12-17 | 26.1 | 27.5 | 53.6 | 27.9 | 29.9 | 57.9 | 28.6 | 29.6 | 58.3 | 21.4 | 22.0 | 43.4 | 31.1 | 32.0 | 63.0 |

TABLE 11   Parental Expenditures on Children by Census Region and Employment Status of Wife, in 1981 Prices
(continued)   (Expenditures in thousands of dollars)

Wife's Employment Status: Not Employed. Three-child Families

| Socioeconomic Status Group | Age Group | Total United States | | | | Northeast | | | | North Central | | | |
|---|---|---|---|---|---|---|---|---|---|---|---|---|---|
| | | First Child | Second Child | Third Child | Total | First Child | Second Child | Third Child | Total | First Child | Second Child | Third Child | Total |
| High | 0-17 | $81.3 | $75.9 | $74.2 | $231.4 | $86.8 | $83.3 | $85.3 | $255.4 | $82.7 | $77.8 | $76.7 | $237.3 |
| | 0-5 | 26.1 | 18.0 | 12.6 | 56.8 | 29.8 | 22.2 | 18.5 | 70.6 | 26.0 | 18.1 | 13.4 | 57.5 |
| | 6-11 | 26.6 | 27.4 | 28.8 | 82.8 | 26.1 | 27.8 | 30.1 | 84.0 | 26.2 | 27.8 | 29.6 | 83.6 |
| | 12-17 | 28.6 | 30.5 | 32.7 | 91.8 | 30.9 | 33.3 | 36.7 | 100.9 | 30.5 | 31.9 | 33.8 | 96.1 |
| Medium | 0-17 | 69.0 | 62.6 | 60.0 | 191.6 | 71.2 | 66.6 | 67.4 | 205.2 | 72.6 | 66.5 | 64.5 | 203.6 |
| | 0-5 | 23.4 | 15.1 | 9.7 | 48.2 | 25.9 | 18.3 | 14.8 | 59.0 | 24.1 | 15.9 | 11.0 | 50.9 |
| | 6-11 | 22.4 | 22.7 | 23.7 | 68.9 | 21.2 | 22.2 | 23.8 | 67.2 | 22.8 | 23.9 | 25.2 | 71.9 |
| | 12-17 | 23.2 | 24.7 | 26.7 | 74.6 | 24.1 | 26.0 | 28.9 | 79.0 | 25.7 | 26.8 | 28.4 | 80.8 |
| Low | 0-17 | 63.3 | 57.0 | 54.6 | 174.9 | 68.1 | 63.5 | 64.4 | 196.0 | 68.0 | 61.8 | 59.6 | 189.4 |
| | 0-5 | 21.6 | 13.5 | 8.3 | 43.4 | 24.9 | 17.5 | 14.0 | 56.3 | 22.8 | 14.7 | 9.9 | 47.5 |
| | 6-11 | 20.5 | 20.8 | 21.7 | 63.0 | 20.2 | 21.1 | 22.6 | 64.0 | 21.4 | 22.3 | 23.4 | 67.1 |
| | 12-17 | 21.2 | 22.7 | 24.6 | 68.5 | 23.0 | 24.9 | 27.8 | 75.7 | 23.8 | 24.8 | 26.3 | 74.9 |

TABLE 11  Parental Expenditures on Children by Census Region and Employment Status of Wife, in 1981 Prices
(continued) (Expenditures in thousands of dollars)

*Wife's Employment Status: Not Employed. Three-child Families*

| Socioeconomic Status Group | Age Group | South | | | | West | | | |
|---|---|---|---|---|---|---|---|---|---|
| | | First Child | Second Child | Third Child | Total | First Child | Second Child | Third Child | Total |
| High | 0-17 | $76.5 | $69.3 | $66.0 | $211.8 | $86.3 | $84.2 | $85.3 | $255.8 |
| | 0-5 | 23.6 | 16.2 | 11.3 | 51.0 | 28.2 | 22.8 | 20.9 | 71.9 |
| | 6-11 | 26.8 | 25.7 | 26.0 | 78.5 | 27.3 | 29.4 | 30.8 | 87.5 |
| | 12-17 | 26.2 | 27.4 | 28.7 | 82.3 | 30.9 | 32.0 | 33.6 | 96.5 |
| Medium | 0-17 | 60.1 | 52.2 | 48.4 | 160.7 | 78.2 | 75.4 | 75.8 | 229.4 |
| | 0-5 | 19.8 | 12.5 | 7.8 | 40.0 | 26.5 | 20.9 | 18.7 | 66.1 |
| | 6-11 | 21.0 | 19.4 | 19.4 | 59.8 | 24.5 | 26.2 | 27.4 | 78.0 |
| | 12-17 | 19.3 | 20.3 | 21.3 | 60.9 | 27.3 | 28.3 | 29.8 | 85.3 |
| Low | 0-17 | 53.1 | 45.8 | 42.6 | 141.5 | 73.0 | 70.3 | 70.7 | 213.9 |
| | 0-5 | 17.5 | 10.7 | 6.3 | 34.5 | 24.8 | 19.4 | 17.2 | 61.4 |
| | 6-11 | 18.5 | 17.0 | 17.0 | 52.5 | 22.7 | 24.4 | 25.6 | 72.7 |
| | 12-17 | 17.1 | 18.1 | 19.3 | 54.5 | 25.4 | 26.4 | 27.9 | 79.8 |

TABLE 12    Parental Expenditures on Children by Residence and Employment Status of Wife, in 1981 Prices
(Expenditures in thousands of dollars)

| Socioeconomic Status Group | Age Group | One-child Families | | | Wife's Employment Status: Full-time, Full-year Worker | | | | | | | | |
| | | | | | Two-child Families | | | | | | | | |
| | | Total United States Total | Metro Total | Non-metro Total | Total United States | | | Metropolitan | | | Nonmetropolitan | | |
| | | | | | First Child | Second Child | Total | First Child | Second Child | Total | First Child | Second Child | Total |
| High | 0–17 | $135.7 | $139.1 | $131.5 | $107.6 | $102.7 | $210.3 | $110.1 | $106.0 | $216.1 | $104.5 | $98.4 | $202.9 |
| | 0–5 | 35.6 | 37.6 | 33.0 | 31.6 | 23.9 | 55.5 | 33.1 | 26.3 | 59.4 | 29.6 | 21.3 | 50.9 |
| | 6–11 | 49.3 | 50.7 | 47.0 | 37.1 | 38.2 | 75.4 | 37.9 | 39.6 | 77.5 | 35.6 | 35.7 | 71.2 |
| | 12–17 | 50.8 | 50.8 | 51.5 | 38.9 | 40.5 | 79.4 | 39.1 | 40.1 | 79.2 | 39.3 | 41.5 | 80.8 |
| Medium | 0–17 | 121.6 | 127.1 | 108.8 | 96.9 | 91.3 | 188.2 | 101.0 | 96.4 | 197.4 | 87.3 | 79.7 | 167.0 |
| | 0–5 | 32.4 | 34.8 | 28.3 | 29.0 | 21.1 | 50.1 | 30.8 | 23.9 | 54.7 | 25.7 | 17.1 | 42.8 |
| | 6–11 | 44.4 | 46.5 | 39.1 | 33.4 | 34.2 | 67.7 | 34.8 | 36.1 | 70.9 | 29.7 | 29.2 | 59.0 |
| | 12–17 | 44.9 | 45.8 | 41.5 | 34.5 | 36.0 | 70.5 | 35.4 | 36.3 | 71.7 | 31.9 | 33.4 | 65.3 |
| Low | 0–17 | 114.7 | 121.7 | 98.1 | 91.6 | 85.9 | 177.5 | 96.8 | 92.2 | 189.1 | 79.0 | 71.5 | 150.5 |
| | 0–5 | 30.6 | 33.4 | 25.4 | 27.5 | 19.7 | 47.2 | 29.6 | 22.8 | 52.4 | 23.3 | 14.8 | 38.1 |
| | 6–11 | 41.9 | 44.6 | 35.3 | 31.6 | 32.3 | 63.9 | 33.3 | 34.7 | 68.0 | 26.9 | 26.3 | 53.2 |
| | 12–17 | 42.2 | 43.7 | 37.4 | 32.5 | 33.9 | 66.4 | 33.9 | 34.7 | 68.6 | 28.8 | 30.3 | 59.2 |

TABLE 12  Parental Expenditures on Children by Residence and Employment Status of Wife, in 1981 Prices
(continued)  (Expenditures in thousands of dollars)

*Wife's Employment Status: Full-time, Full-year Worker, Three-child Families*

| Socioeconomic Status Group | Age Group | Total United States | | | | Metropolitan | | | | Nonmetropolitan | | | |
|---|---|---|---|---|---|---|---|---|---|---|---|---|---|
| | | First Child | Second Child | Third Child | Total | First Child | Second Child | Third Child | Total | First Child | Second Child | Third Child | Total |
| High | 0-17 | $93.5 | $86.1 | $83.1 | $262.7 | $95.2 | $88.6 | $86.6 | $270.4 | $91.5 | $82.8 | $78.1 | $252.5 |
| | 0-5 | 32.0 | 22.4 | 16.0 | 70.4 | 33.3 | 24.2 | 18.9 | 76.4 | 30.3 | 20.3 | 13.0 | 63.6 |
| | 6-11 | 30.2 | 30.7 | 31.9 | 92.8 | 30.3 | 31.5 | 33.2 | 95.0 | 29.3 | 28.8 | 28.9 | 87.1 |
| | 12-17 | 31.3 | 33.0 | 35.2 | 99.4 | 31.6 | 32.9 | 34.5 | 99.0 | 32.0 | 33.7 | 36.2 | 101.8 |
| Medium | 0-17 | 84.6 | 76.8 | 73.5 | 234.9 | 87.6 | 80.8 | 78.5 | 246.9 | 77.2 | 67.7 | 62.1 | 207.0 |
| | 0-5 | 29.5 | 20.0 | 13.7 | 63.1 | 31.1 | 22.1 | 16.9 | 70.1 | 26.6 | 16.7 | 9.2 | 52.5 |
| | 6-11 | 27.3 | 27.5 | 28.5 | 83.2 | 27.8 | 28.8 | 30.3 | 86.9 | 24.6 | 23.7 | 23.5 | 71.9 |
| | 12-17 | 27.8 | 29.4 | 31.4 | 88.6 | 28.7 | 29.9 | 31.4 | 90.0 | 26.0 | 27.3 | 29.4 | 82.7 |
| Low | 0-17 | 80.1 | 72.4 | 69.1 | 221.6 | 84.1 | 77.4 | 75.1 | 236.6 | 70.3 | 60.9 | 55.5 | 186.7 |
| | 0-5 | 28.0 | 18.7 | 12.5 | 59.2 | 30.0 | 21.1 | 15.9 | 67.0 | 24.3 | 14.7 | 7.4 | 46.4 |
| | 6-11 | 25.8 | 26.0 | 26.9 | 78.7 | 26.7 | 27.6 | 29.0 | 83.3 | 22.4 | 21.4 | 21.2 | 65.0 |
| | 12-17 | 26.2 | 27.7 | 29.7 | 83.7 | 27.5 | 28.6 | 30.2 | 86.3 | 23.6 | 24.8 | 26.9 | 75.3 |

TABLE 13   Parental Expenditures on Children by Residence and Employment Status of Wife, in 1981 Prices
(Expenditures in thousands of dollars)

| | | One-child Families | | | Two-child Families | | | | | | | | |
| | | | | | Wife's Employment Status: Not Employed | | | | | | | | |
| | | | | | Total United States | | | Metropolitan | | | Nonmetropolitan | | |
| Socioeconomic Status Group | Age Group | Total United States Total | Metro Total | Non-metro Total | First Child | Second Child | Total | First Child | Second Child | Total | First Child | Second Child | Total |
|---|---|---|---|---|---|---|---|---|---|---|---|---|---|
| High | 0–17 | $117.8 | $123.5 | $101.8 | $93.5 | $90.5 | $184.0 | $97.7 | $95.9 | $193.6 | $81.6 | $75.6 | $157.2 |
| | 0–5 | 28.4 | 30.6 | 24.5 | 25.5 | 19.0 | 44.5 | 27.1 | 21.7 | 48.8 | 22.5 | 14.7 | 37.3 |
| | 6–11 | 43.2 | 45.4 | 36.7 | 32.6 | 34.1 | 66.7 | 33.9 | 36.1 | 70.1 | 27.9 | 27.9 | 55.8 |
| | 12–17 | 46.2 | 47.5 | 40.5 | 35.5 | 37.4 | 72.8 | 36.6 | 38.0 | 74.7 | 31.2 | 33.0 | 64.2 |
| Medium | 0–17 | 98.3 | 103.6 | 86.4 | 78.7 | 74.0 | 152.8 | 82.7 | 79.1 | 161.8 | 70.0 | 62.9 | 132.9 |
| | 0–5 | 24.9 | 27.2 | 21.7 | 22.7 | 15.7 | 38.4 | 24.3 | 18.4 | 42.8 | 20.1 | 12.1 | 32.3 |
| | 6–11 | 36.3 | 38.4 | 31.4 | 27.4 | 28.3 | 55.7 | 28.7 | 30.1 | 58.8 | 24.0 | 23.5 | 47.4 |
| | 12–17 | 37.1 | 47.1 | 33.4 | 28.7 | 30.1 | 58.7 | 29.7 | 30.6 | 60.2 | 25.9 | 27.3 | 53.2 |
| Low | 0–17 | 89.5 | 95.4 | 78.8 | 72.0 | 67.3 | 139.2 | 76.3 | 72.7 | 149.0 | 64.1 | 57.1 | 121.3 |
| | 0–5 | 22.7 | 25.1 | 19.6 | 20.8 | 14.0 | 34.7 | 22.5 | 16.8 | 39.3 | 18.4 | 10.5 | 28.9 |
| | 6–11 | 33.2 | 35.4 | 28.6 | 25.1 | 25.8 | 50.9 | 26.5 | 27.8 | 54.2 | 21.9 | 21.4 | 43.4 |
| | 12–17 | 33.6 | 34.8 | 30.6 | 26.1 | 27.5 | 53.6 | 27.3 | 28.2 | 55.5 | 23.8 | 25.2 | 49.0 |

TABLE 13   Parental Expenditures on Children by Residence and Employment Status of Wife, in 1981 Prices
(continued)   (Expenditures in thousands of dollars)

Wife's Employment Status: Not Employed, Three-child Families

| Socioeconomic Status Group | Age Group | Total United States | | | | Metropolitan | | | | Nonmetropolitan | | | |
|---|---|---|---|---|---|---|---|---|---|---|---|---|---|
| | | First Child | Second Child | Third Child | Total | First Child | Second Child | Third Child | Total | First Child | Second Child | Third Child | Total |
| High | 0–17 | $81.3 | $75.9 | $74.2 | $231.4 | $84.3 | $80.1 | $79.7 | $244.1 | $72.2 | $64.2 | $59.7 | $196.1 |
| | 0–5 | 26.1 | 18.0 | 12.6 | 56.8 | 27.5 | 20.1 | 15.9 | 63.5 | 23.5 | 14.6 | 7.8 | 45.9 |
| | 6–11 | 26.6 | 27.4 | 28.8 | 82.8 | 27.2 | 28.8 | 30.8 | 86.8 | 23.2 | 22.6 | 22.7 | 68.5 |
| | 12–17 | 28.6 | 30.5 | 32.7 | 91.8 | 29.7 | 31.2 | 33.0 | 93.9 | 25.4 | 27.0 | 29.3 | 81.7 |
| Medium | 0–17 | 69.0 | 62.6 | 60.0 | 191.6 | 71.9 | 66.5 | 65.1 | 203.5 | 62.5 | 53.8 | 48.8 | 165.1 |
| | 0–5 | 23.4 | 15.1 | 9.7 | 48.2 | 24.8 | 17.2 | 12.8 | 54.8 | 21.3 | 12.3 | 5.5 | 39.0 |
| | 6–11 | 22.4 | 22.7 | 23.7 | 68.9 | 23.0 | 24.0 | 25.5 | 72.4 | 20.0 | 19.1 | 18.9 | 58.1 |
| | 12–17 | 23.2 | 24.7 | 26.7 | 74.6 | 24.1 | 25.3 | 26.8 | 76.3 | 21.2 | 22.4 | 24.4 | 68.1 |
| Low | 0–17 | 63.3 | 57.0 | 54.6 | 174.9 | 66.6 | 61.3 | 59.9 | 187.8 | 57.5 | 49.1 | 44.4 | 150.9 |
| | 0–5 | 21.6 | 13.5 | 8.3 | 43.4 | 23.1 | 15.7 | 11.4 | 50.2 | 19.6 | 10.8 | 4.3 | 34.7 |
| | 6–11 | 20.5 | 20.8 | 21.7 | 63.0 | 21.2 | 22.1 | 23.5 | 66.8 | 18.3 | 17.5 | 17.3 | 53.2 |
| | 12–17 | 21.2 | 22.7 | 24.6 | 68.5 | 22.3 | 23.5 | 25.0 | 70.7 | 19.6 | 20.8 | 22.8 | 63.1 |

TABLE 14 Parental Expenditures on Children, Age 0–17, by Expenditure Category and Employment Status of Wife, in 1981 Prices (Expenditures in thousands of dollars)

| | | | | Wife's Employment Status: Full-time, Full-year Worker | | | | | | | | |
| | | One-child Families | | Two-child Families | | | | Three-child Families | | | | | |
| | | Total | | First Child | | Second Child | | First Child | | Second Child | | Third Child | |
| Socioeconomic Status Group | Expenditure Category | ($) | (%) | ($) | (%) | ($) | (%) | ($) | (%) | ($) | (%) | ($) | (%) |
|---|---|---|---|---|---|---|---|---|---|---|---|---|---|
| High | Food at home | 18.9 | 13.9 | 16.8 | 15.6 | 16.2 | 15.8 | 15.8 | 16.9 | 15.0 | 17.4 | 14.6 | 17.6 |
| | Food away from home | 6.7 | 4.9 | 5.2 | 4.8 | 4.7 | 4.6 | 4.4 | 4.7 | 3.8 | 4.4 | 3.5 | 4.2 |
| | Shelter | 16.3 | 12.0 | 10.7 | 9.9 | 12.9 | 12.6 | 8.4 | 9.0 | 9.3 | 10.8 | 11.0 | 13.2 |
| | Fuel and utilities | 5.3 | 3.9 | 4.6 | 4.3 | 4.3 | 4.2 | 4.2 | 4.5 | 3.9 | 4.5 | 3.8 | 4.6 |
| | Household goods | 13.8 | 10.2 | 11.1 | 10.3 | 10.3 | 10.0 | 9.7 | 10.4 | 8.7 | 10.1 | 8.1 | 9.7 |
| | Clothing | 9.6 | 7.1 | 7.8 | 7.2 | 7.3 | 7.1 | 6.9 | 7.4 | 6.2 | 7.2 | 5.9 | 7.1 |
| | Transportation | 36.0 | 26.5 | 28.3 | 26.3 | 25.8 | 25.1 | 24.3 | 26.0 | 21.3 | 24.7 | 19.6 | 23.6 |
| | Health care | 7.4 | 5.5 | 6.0 | 5.6 | 5.7 | 5.6 | 5.3 | 5.7 | 4.9 | 5.7 | 4.7 | 5.7 |
| | Recreation | 13.7 | 10.1 | 10.8 | 10.0 | 9.8 | 9.5 | 9.2 | 9.8 | 8.2 | 9.5 | 7.5 | 9.0 |
| | Miscellaneous | 8.0 | 5.9 | 6.3 | 5.9 | 5.8 | 5.6 | 5.4 | 5.8 | 4.8 | 5.6 | 4.5 | 5.4 |
| | Total | 135.7 | 100.0 | 107.6 | 100.0 | 102.7 | 100.0 | 93.5 | 100.0 | 86.1 | 100.0 | 83.1 | 100.0 |
| Medium | Food at home | 17.9 | 14.7 | 16.0 | 16.5 | 15.4 | 16.9 | 15.1 | 17.8 | 14.3 | 18.6 | 13.9 | 18.9 |
| | Food away from home | 6.0 | 4.9 | 4.6 | 4.7 | 4.1 | 4.5 | 3.9 | 4.6 | 3.3 | 4.3 | 3.0 | 4.1 |
| | Shelter | 13.4 | 11.0 | 8.9 | 9.2 | 10.4 | 11.4 | 7.0 | 8.3 | 7.5 | 9.8 | 8.7 | 11.8 |
| | Fuel and utilities | 4.7 | 3.9 | 4.3 | 4.4 | 4.1 | 4.5 | 4.0 | 4.7 | 3.7 | 4.8 | 3.6 | 4.9 |
| | Household goods | 12.5 | 10.3 | 10.0 | 10.3 | 9.2 | 10.1 | 8.8 | 10.4 | 7.8 | 10.2 | 7.2 | 9.8 |
| | Clothing | 8.7 | 7.2 | 7.1 | 7.3 | 6.6 | 7.2 | 6.3 | 7.4 | 5.6 | 7.3 | 5.3 | 7.2 |
| | Transportation | 32.2 | 26.5 | 25.3 | 26.1 | 22.7 | 24.9 | 21.7 | 25.7 | 18.8 | 24.5 | 17.2 | 23.4 |
| | Health care | 6.7 | 5.5 | 5.5 | 5.7 | 5.1 | 5.6 | 4.8 | 5.7 | 4.4 | 5.7 | 4.2 | 5.7 |
| | Recreation | 12.3 | 10.1 | 9.6 | 9.9 | 8.7 | 9.5 | 8.3 | 9.8 | 7.2 | 9.4 | 6.6 | 9.0 |
| | Miscellaneous | 7.1 | 5.8 | 5.6 | 5.8 | 5.1 | 5.6 | 4.8 | 5.7 | 4.2 | 5.5 | 3.9 | 5.3 |
| | Total | 121.6 | 100.0 | 96.9 | 100.0 | 91.3 | 100.0 | 84.6 | 100.0 | 76.8 | 100.0 | 73.5 | 100.0 |

TABLE 14  Parental Expenditures on Children, Age 0–17, by Expenditure Category and Employment Status of Wife, in 1981 Prices
*(continued)*  *(Expenditures in thousands of dollars)*

| | | One-child Families Total | | Two-child Families | | | | Three-child Families | | | | | |
| | | | | First Child | | Second Child | | First Child | | Second Child | | Third Child | |
| Socioeconomic Status Group | Expenditure Category | ($) | (%) | ($) | (%) | ($) | (%) | ($) | (%) | ($) | (%) | ($) | (%) |
|---|---|---|---|---|---|---|---|---|---|---|---|---|---|
| Low | Food at home | 17.4 | 15.2 | 15.6 | 17.0 | 15.0 | 17.5 | 14.8 | 18.5 | 14.0 | 19.3 | 13.6 | 19.7 |
| | Food away from home | 5.6 | 4.9 | 4.3 | 4.7 | 3.8 | 4.4 | 3.6 | 4.5 | 3.1 | 4.3 | 2.7 | 3.9 |
| | Shelter | 12.0 | 10.5 | 8.0 | 8.7 | 9.3 | 10.8 | 6.3 | 7.9 | 6.7 | 9.3 | 7.7 | 11.1 |
| | Fuel and utilities | 4.7 | 4.1 | 4.2 | 4.6 | 3.9 | 4.5 | 3.9 | 4.9 | 3.6 | 5.0 | 3.5 | 5.1 |
| | Household goods | 11.8 | 10.3 | 9.5 | 10.4 | 8.7 | 10.1 | 8.3 | 10.4 | 7.2 | 9.9 | 6.8 | 9.8 |
| | Clothing | 8.3 | 7.2 | 6.8 | 7.4 | 6.2 | 7.2 | 6.0 | 7.5 | 5.4 | 7.5 | 5.0 | 7.2 |
| | Transportation | 30.3 | 26.4 | 23.7 | 25.9 | 21.3 | 24.8 | 20.4 | 25.5 | 17.5 | 24.2 | 16.0 | 23.2 |
| | Health care | 6.4 | 5.6 | 5.2 | 5.7 | 4.9 | 5.7 | 4.6 | 5.7 | 4.2 | 5.8 | 4.0 | 5.8 |
| | Recreation | 11.5 | 10.0 | 9.0 | 9.8 | 8.1 | 9.4 | 7.8 | 9.7 | 6.7 | 9.3 | 6.1 | 8.8 |
| | Miscellaneous | 6.7 | 5.8 | 5.3 | 5.8 | 4.8 | 5.6 | 4.5 | 5.6 | 4.0 | 5.5 | 3.6 | 5.2 |
| | Total | 114.7 | 100.0 | 91.6 | 100.0 | 85.9 | 100.0 | 80.1 | 100.0 | 72.4 | 100.0 | 69.1 | 100.0 |

*Wife's Employment Status: Full-time, Full-year Worker*

TABLE 15   Parental Expenditures on Children, Age 0–17, by Expenditure Category and Employment Status of Wife, in 1981 Prices
(Expenditures in thousands of dollars)

| Socioeconomic Status Group | Expenditure Category | One-child Families Total | | Wife's Employment Status: Part-time, Full-year Worker | | | | | | | | |
|---|---|---|---|---|---|---|---|---|---|---|---|---|
| | | | | Two-child Families | | | | Three-child Families | | | | | |
| | | | | First Child | | Second Child | | First Child | | Second Child | | Third Child | |
| | | ($) | (%) | ($) | (%) | ($) | (%) | ($) | (%) | ($) | (%) | ($) | (%) |
| High | Food at home | 18.2 | 14.4 | 16.3 | 16.3 | 15.7 | 16.3 | 15.3 | 17.6 | 14.6 | 18.1 | 14.2 | 18.1 |
| | Food away from home | 6.2 | 4.9 | 4.8 | 4.8 | 4.3 | 4.5 | 4.0 | 4.6 | 3.5 | 4.3 | 3.2 | 4.1 |
| | Shelter | 14.4 | 11.4 | 9.4 | 9.4 | 11.6 | 12.0 | 7.3 | 8.4 | 8.3 | 10.3 | 9.9 | 12.6 |
| | Fuel and utilities | 5.0 | 4.0 | 4.4 | 4.4 | 4.2 | 4.4 | 4.0 | 4.6 | 3.8 | 4.7 | 3.7 | 4.7 |
| | Household goods | 12.9 | 10.2 | 10.4 | 10.4 | 9.6 | 10.0 | 9.0 | 10.3 | 8.2 | 10.1 | 7.7 | 9.8 |
| | Clothing | 9.0 | 7.1 | 7.3 | 7.3 | 6.9 | 7.2 | 6.5 | 7.5 | 5.9 | 7.3 | 5.6 | 7.1 |
| | Transportation | 33.5 | 26.5 | 26.2 | 26.1 | 24.1 | 25.0 | 22.4 | 25.7 | 19.9 | 24.6 | 18.5 | 23.5 |
| | Health care | 6.9 | 5.5 | 5.6 | 5.6 | 5.4 | 5.6 | 5.0 | 5.7 | 4.6 | 5.7 | 4.5 | 5.7 |
| | Recreation | 12.7 | 10.1 | 10.0 | 10.0 | 9.2 | 9.5 | 8.5 | 9.8 | 7.6 | 9.4 | 7.1 | 9.0 |
| | Miscellaneous | 7.4 | 5.9 | 5.8 | 5.8 | 5.4 | 5.6 | 5.0 | 5.7 | 4.5 | 5.6 | 4.2 | 5.3 |
| | Total | 126.3 | 100.0 | 100.2 | 100.0 | 96.4 | 100.0 | 87.1 | 100.0 | 80.8 | 100.0 | 78.6 | 100.0 |
| Medium | Food at home | 16.7 | 15.7 | 15.1 | 17.8 | 14.6 | 18.3 | 14.3 | 19.2 | 13.6 | 20.2 | 13.3 | 20.6 |
| | Food away from home | 5.1 | 4.8 | 3.9 | 4.6 | 3.5 | 4.4 | 3.3 | 4.4 | 2.8 | 4.2 | 2.5 | 3.9 |
| | Shelter | 10.5 | 9.9 | 6.9 | 8.1 | 8.1 | 10.1 | 5.5 | 7.4 | 5.8 | 8.6 | 6.8 | 10.5 |
| | Fuel and utilities | 4.5 | 4.2 | 4.0 | 4.7 | 3.8 | 4.8 | 3.7 | 5.0 | 3.5 | 5.2 | 3.3 | 5.1 |
| | Household goods | 11.0 | 10.4 | 8.8 | 10.4 | 8.1 | 10.1 | 7.7 | 10.4 | 6.8 | 10.1 | 6.4 | 9.9 |
| | Clothing | 7.7 | 7.3 | 6.3 | 7.4 | 5.8 | 7.3 | 5.6 | 7.5 | 5.0 | 7.4 | 4.7 | 7.3 |
| | Transportation | 27.9 | 26.3 | 21.8 | 25.7 | 19.6 | 24.5 | 18.7 | 25.2 | 16.1 | 23.9 | 14.8 | 22.9 |
| | Health care | 5.9 | 5.6 | 4.8 | 5.7 | 4.6 | 5.8 | 4.3 | 5.8 | 3.9 | 5.8 | 3.8 | 5.9 |
| | Recreation | 10.6 | 10.0 | 8.3 | 9.8 | 7.5 | 9.4 | 7.1 | 9.6 | 6.2 | 9.2 | 5.7 | 8.8 |
| | Miscellaneous | 6.2 | 5.8 | 4.9 | 5.8 | 4.4 | 5.5 | 4.2 | 5.7 | 3.6 | 5.3 | 3.4 | 5.3 |
| | Total | 106.2 | 100.0 | 84.9 | 100.0 | 80.0 | 100.0 | 74.3 | 100.0 | 67.4 | 100.0 | 64.7 | 100.0 |

TABLE 15 Parental Expenditures on Children, Age 0–17, by Expenditure Category and Employment Status of Wife, in 1981 Prices
(continued) (Expenditures in thousands of dollars)

| | | | | Wife's Employment Status: Part-time, Full-year Worker | | | | | | | | | |
| | | One-child Families | | Two-child Families | | | | Three-child Families | | | | | |
| | | Total | | First Child | | Second Child | | First Child | | Second Child | | Third Child | |
| Socioeconomic Status Group | Expenditure Category | ($) | (%) | ($) | (%) | ($) | (%) | ($) | (%) | ($) | (%) | ($) | (%) |
|---|---|---|---|---|---|---|---|---|---|---|---|---|---|
| Low | Food at home | 16.0 | 16.6 | 14.6 | 18.8 | 14.0 | 19.3 | 13.8 | 20.3 | 13.2 | 21.5 | 12.8 | 21.8 |
| | Food away from home | 4.6 | 4.8 | 3.5 | 4.5 | 3.1 | 4.3 | 2.9 | 4.3 | 2.4 | 3.9 | 2.2 | 3.8 |
| | Shelter | 8.8 | 9.1 | 5.8 | 7.5 | 6.7 | 9.2 | 4.6 | 6.8 | 4.8 | 7.8 | 5.7 | 9.7 |
| | Fuel and utilities | 4.3 | 4.4 | 3.8 | 4.9 | 3.6 | 5.0 | 3.5 | 5.1 | 3.3 | 5.4 | 3.2 | 5.5 |
| | Household goods | 10.0 | 10.4 | 8.0 | 10.3 | 7.3 | 10.1 | 7.1 | 10.4 | 6.2 | 10.1 | 5.8 | 9.9 |
| | Clothing | 7.1 | 7.3 | 5.8 | 7.5 | 5.4 | 7.4 | 5.2 | 7.6 | 4.6 | 7.5 | 4.4 | 7.5 |
| | Transportation | 25.2 | 26.1 | 19.6 | 25.3 | 17.5 | 24.1 | 16.8 | 24.7 | 14.4 | 23.5 | 13.1 | 22.4 |
| | Health care | 5.4 | 5.6 | 4.5 | 5.8 | 4.2 | 5.8 | 4.0 | 5.9 | 3.6 | 5.9 | 3.5 | 6.0 |
| | Recreation | 9.6 | 9.9 | 7.5 | 9.7 | 6.7 | 9.2 | 6.4 | 9.4 | 5.5 | 9.0 | 5.0 | 8.5 |
| | Miscellaneous | 5.6 | 5.8 | 4.4 | 5.7 | 4.0 | 5.5 | 3.8 | 5.6 | 3.3 | 5.4 | 3.0 | 5.1 |
| | Total | 96.6 | 100.0 | 77.5 | 100.0 | 72.5 | 100.0 | 68.0 | 100.0 | 61.3 | 100.0 | 58.6 | 100.0 |

TABLE 16   Parental Expenditures on Children, Age 0–17, by Expenditure Category and Employment Status of Wife, in 1981 Prices (Expenditures in thousands of dollars)

| | | One-child Families | | Two-child Families | | | | Three-child Families | | | | | |
| | | Total | | First Child | | Second Child | | First Child | | Second Child | | Third Child | |
| Socioeconomic Status Group | Expenditure Category | ($) | (%) | ($) | (%) | ($) | (%) | ($) | (%) | ($) | (%) | ($) | (%) |
|---|---|---|---|---|---|---|---|---|---|---|---|---|---|
| High | Food at home | 17.6 | 14.9 | 15.8 | 16.9 | 15.3 | 16.9 | 14.9 | 18.3 | 14.3 | 18.8 | 13.9 | 18.7 |
| | Food away from home | 5.7 | 4.8 | 4.4 | 4.7 | 4.0 | 4.4 | 3.7 | 4.6 | 3.2 | 4.2 | 3.0 | 4.0 |
| | Shelter | 12.7 | 10.8 | 8.3 | 8.9 | 10.3 | 11.4 | 6.4 | 7.9 | 7.4 | 9.7 | 9.0 | 12.1 |
| | Fuel and utilities | 4.8 | 4.1 | 4.2 | 4.5 | 4.0 | 4.4 | 4.0 | 4.9 | 3.7 | 4.9 | 3.6 | 4.9 |
| | Household goods | 12.1 | 10.3 | 9.7 | 10.4 | 9.1 | 10.1 | 8.4 | 10.3 | 7.7 | 10.1 | 7.3 | 9.8 |
| | Clothing | 8.5 | 7.2 | 6.9 | 7.4 | 6.5 | 7.2 | 6.1 | 7.5 | 5.6 | 7.4 | 5.3 | 7.1 |
| | Transportation | 31.1 | 26.4 | 24.3 | 26.0 | 22.5 | 24.9 | 20.7 | 25.5 | 18.5 | 24.4 | 17.3 | 23.3 |
| | Health care | 6.5 | 5.5 | 5.3 | 5.7 | 5.1 | 5.6 | 4.7 | 5.8 | 4.4 | 5.8 | 4.2 | 5.7 |
| | Recreation | 11.8 | 10.0 | 9.3 | 9.9 | 8.6 | 9.5 | 7.8 | 9.6 | 7.1 | 9.4 | 6.6 | 8.9 |
| | Miscellaneous | 6.9 | 5.9 | 5.4 | 5.8 | 5.0 | 5.5 | 4.6 | 5.7 | 4.2 | 5.5 | 3.9 | 5.3 |
| | Total | 117.8 | 100.0 | 93.5 | 100.0 | 90.5 | 100.0 | 81.3 | 100.0 | 75.9 | 100.0 | 74.2 | 100.0 |
| Medium | Food at home | 16.1 | 16.4 | 14.7 | 18.7 | 14.1 | 19.1 | 13.9 | 20.1 | 13.3 | 21.2 | 12.9 | 21.5 |
| | Food away from home | 4.7 | 4.8 | 3.5 | 4.4 | 3.1 | 4.2 | 3.0 | 4.3 | 2.5 | 4.0 | 2.3 | 3.8 |
| | Shelter | 9.1 | 9.3 | 6.0 | 7.6 | 7.0 | 9.5 | 4.7 | 6.8 | 5.0 | 8.0 | 5.9 | 9.8 |
| | Fuel and utilities | 4.3 | 4.4 | 3.8 | 4.8 | 3.6 | 4.9 | 3.6 | 5.2 | 3.3 | 5.3 | 3.2 | 5.3 |
| | Household goods | 10.2 | 10.4 | 8.2 | 10.4 | 7.5 | 10.1 | 7.2 | 10.4 | 6.3 | 10.1 | 5.9 | 9.8 |
| | Clothing | 7.2 | 7.3 | 5.9 | 7.5 | 5.5 | 7.4 | 5.2 | 7.5 | 4.7 | 7.5 | 4.4 | 7.3 |
| | Transportation | 25.7 | 26.1 | 20.0 | 25.4 | 18.0 | 24.3 | 17.1 | 24.8 | 14.7 | 23.5 | 13.5 | 22.5 |
| | Health care | 5.5 | 5.6 | 4.5 | 5.7 | 4.3 | 5.8 | 4.0 | 5.8 | 3.7 | 5.9 | 3.5 | 5.8 |
| | Recreation | 9.8 | 10.0 | 7.6 | 9.7 | 6.9 | 9.3 | 6.5 | 9.4 | 5.6 | 8.9 | 5.2 | 8.7 |
| | Miscellaneous | 5.7 | 5.8 | 4.5 | 5.7 | 4.0 | 5.4 | 3.8 | 5.5 | 3.3 | 5.3 | 3.1 | 5.2 |
| | Total | 98.3 | 100.0 | 78.7 | 100.0 | 74.0 | 100.0 | 69.0 | 100.0 | 62.6 | 100.0 | 60.0 | 100.0 |

*Wife's Employment Status: Not Employed*

TABLE 16 Parental Expenditures on Children, Age 0–17, by Expenditure Category and Employment Status of Wife, in 1981 Prices
(*continued*) (*Expenditures in thousands of dollars*)

| | | One-child Families | | Two-child Families | | | | Three-child Families | | | | | |
| | | | | First Child | | Second Child | | First Child | | Second Child | | Third Child | |
| Socioeconomic Status Group | Expenditure Category | ($) | (%) | ($) | (%) | ($) | (%) | ($) | (%) | ($) | (%) | ($) | (%) |
|---|---|---|---|---|---|---|---|---|---|---|---|---|---|
| Low | Food at home | 15.5 | 17.3 | 14.1 | 19.6 | 13.6 | 20.2 | 13.5 | 21.3 | 12.8 | 22.5 | 12.5 | 22.9 |
| | Food away from home | 4.2 | 4.7 | 3.1 | 4.3 | 2.8 | 4.2 | 2.6 | 4.1 | 2.2 | 3.9 | 2.0 | 3.7 |
| | Shelter | 7.7 | 8.6 | 5.1 | 7.1 | 5.8 | 8.6 | 4.0 | 6.3 | 4.2 | 7.4 | 4.9 | 9.0 |
| | Fuel and utilities | 4.1 | 4.6 | 3.6 | 5.0 | 3.5 | 5.2 | 3.4 | 5.4 | 3.2 | 5.6 | 3.1 | 5.7 |
| | Household goods | 9.3 | 10.4 | 7.5 | 10.4 | 6.8 | 10.1 | 6.6 | 10.4 | 5.9 | 10.4 | 5.4 | 9.9 |
| | Clothing | 6.6 | 7.4 | 5.4 | 7.5 | 5.0 | 7.4 | 4.8 | 7.6 | 4.3 | 7.5 | 4.1 | 7.5 |
| | Transportation | 23.2 | 25.9 | 18.0 | 25.0 | 16.1 | 23.9 | 15.4 | 24.3 | 13.1 | 23.0 | 12.0 | 22.0 |
| | Health care | 5.1 | 5.7 | 4.2 | 5.8 | 3.9 | 5.8 | 3.7 | 5.8 | 3.4 | 6.0 | 3.3 | 6.0 |
| | Recreation | 8.8 | 9.8 | 6.9 | 9.6 | 6.1 | 9.1 | 5.9 | 9.3 | 5.0 | 8.8 | 4.6 | 8.4 |
| | Miscellaneous | 5.1 | 5.7 | 4.0 | 5.6 | 3.6 | 5.3 | 3.5 | 5.5 | 3.0 | 5.3 | 2.8 | 5.1 |
| | Total | 89.5 | 100.0 | 72.0 | 100.0 | 67.3 | 100.0 | 63.3 | 100.0 | 57.0 | 100.0 | 54.6 | 100.0 |

*Wife's Employment Status: Not Employed*

transportation for children is the high cost of owning and maintaining an automobile. Between 1972–1973 and 1981, prices of transportation-related goods and services increased by over 130 percent (see table 2). Looking at the same family, $14,850 or 18 percent of the average child's total budget is spent on food at home. Thus, expenses for transportation and food at home comprise between 40 and 45 percent of the average child's total budget to age 18. Allocations per child for other expenditure components are as follows: household goods, 10.3 percent; recreation 9.6 percent; shelter, 9.1 percent; clothing, 7.3 percent; health care, 5.7 percent; miscellaneous, 5.6 percent; fuel and utilities, 4.7 percent; and food away from home, 4.5 percent.

Comparing child-related expenditure patterns across income levels highlights an interesting finding about expenses associated with food at home. Expenditures for food at home consistently rank second, behind transportation costs, regardless of income level. However, although the actual dollar amount spent by parents on food at home for their children drops as one moves from the higher to the lower income levels, the percentage share of total expenses devoted to food at home rises. Returning to the two-child family in the high SES group, where the wife works part time, we see that $16,000 or 16.3 percent of the total budget for an average child is spent on food at home. At the medium SES level, the corresponding dollar figure is less ($14,900), but it is a larger share of the budget (18.1 percent). For the low SES family, the corresponding figures are $14,300 and 19.1 percent. The same pattern appears when comparisons are made across variations in wife's employment status. Families with a working wife (and therefore with more income) spend more in absolute dollars on their children's food at home than families where the wife does not work for pay, but these larger expenditures comprise a smaller share of the child's total budget. Consequently, what is true for families also holds for individual children; a decline in the proportion of the total budget allocated to food at home corresponds to a rising material standard of living.

The categories we have shown separately as food at home and food away from home are often collapsed into a single group, total food. Likewise, expenses for shelter, fuel and utilities, and household goods compose total housing expenditures. Viewed in this way, transportation continues to be the most important item of expense in the eldest child's budget, followed next by housing and then food. For children other than the eldest, the general pattern favors housing as the most important expenditure category, followed by transportation and food in that order. Exceptions to this overall picture arise in medium and low SES families where the mother is not working. These families presumably have among the lowest standards of living, other things (including family size) held constant. In such families with two or three children, more is spent on children for food than for any other item. Housing and transportation expenditures are approximately tied for second place.

Data from the Health Care Financing Administration (HCFA) permit an independent check on one aspect of our estimates. HCFA compiles statistics for personal health care expenditures on a regular basis. According to HCFA estimates, annual health care expenditures per child averaged $104.77 in 1970 and $165.19 in 1976.[2] In uninflated 1972-1973 prices, we estimate that two-child families at the medium SES level and in which the wife works part time would devote $2,170 to health care expenditures in rearing the average child to age 18. Dividing this total by 18 yields $120.55 per year. Since this annual figure lies between the HCFA estimates for 1970 and 1976, we conclude that we can have greater confidence in the accuracy of our overall estimates.

## Effects of Spacing and Timing of Births

At the beginning of this chapter we stated that our estimates of expenditures on children in two- and three-child families were based on the assumption of a two-year interval between children. Because all families do not space their children two years apart, it is useful to alter this assumption and examine the results for possible effects of variations in the birth interval between children.

### Spacing

The data presented in table 17 are estimates of the expected level of parental expenditures for each child in a two-child family where the wife works part time. Results are shown for each of four possible spacing intervals ranging between one and four years. Estimates have been computed for both the first and second child, broken down by the age of the child and by the family income level.

Postponing the birth of the second child an additional year increases the total amount devoted to child-related expenditures, although these increases are not striking. Parents who wait only one year to have a second child spend the smallest amount per child while parents who delay the

TABLE 17   Parental Expenditures on Children by Birth Interval between Children, Total United States, 1981 Prices
*(Expenditures in thousands of dollars)*

| | | Wife's Employment Status: Part-time, Full-year Worker, Birth Interval Between Children | | | | | | | | | | | | |
| | | 1 Year | | | 2 Years | | | 3 Years | | | 4 Years | | |
| Socioeconomic Status Group | Age Group | First Child | Second Child | Total | First Child | Second Child | Total | First Child | Second Child | Total | First Child | Second Child | Total |
|---|---|---|---|---|---|---|---|---|---|---|---|---|---|
| High | 0–17 | $99.1 | $94.4 | $193.5 | $100.2 | $96.4 | $196.6 | $101.3 | $98.2 | $199.5 | $103.0 | $99.8 | $202.8 |
| | 0–5 | 26.6 | 20.7 | 47.3 | 28.3 | 21.3 | 49.5 | 29.9 | 21.8 | 51.7 | 31.2 | 22.4 | 53.6 |
| | 6–11 | 34.9 | 35.7 | 70.5 | 34.8 | 36.1 | 70.9 | 34.6 | 36.6 | 71.2 | 35.1 | 37.0 | 72.1 |
| | 12–17 | 37.7 | 38.1 | 75.7 | 37.2 | 39.0 | 76.2 | 36.7 | 39.8 | 76.6 | 36.6 | 40.4 | 77.0 |
| Medium | 0–17 | 84.0 | 78.7 | 162.6 | 84.9 | 80.0 | 164.8 | 85.7 | 81.3 | 167.0 | 87.2 | 82.3 | 169.5 |
| | 0–5 | 23.3 | 17.2 | 40.4 | 24.7 | 17.5 | 42.2 | 26.1 | 17.9 | 44.0 | 27.2 | 18.2 | 45.4 |
| | 6–11 | 29.5 | 30.1 | 59.6 | 29.4 | 30.3 | 59.7 | 29.3 | 30.5 | 59.9 | 29.8 | 30.8 | 60.6 |
| | 12–17 | 31.2 | 31.4 | 62.5 | 30.7 | 32.2 | 62.9 | 30.3 | 32.9 | 63.1 | 30.2 | 33.4 | 63.5 |
| Low | 0–17 | 76.7 | 71.3 | 148.0 | 77.5 | 72.5 | 149.9 | 78.2 | 73.7 | 151.9 | 79.5 | 74.6 | 154.2 |
| | 0–5 | 21.3 | 15.3 | 36.6 | 22.6 | 15.5 | 38.2 | 23.9 | 15.8 | 39.8 | 24.9 | 16.1 | 41.0 |
| | 6–11 | 27.0 | 27.5 | 54.5 | 26.9 | 27.6 | 54.5 | 26.8 | 27.8 | 54.6 | 27.2 | 28.1 | 55.3 |
| | 12–17 | 28.4 | 28.6 | 56.9 | 27.9 | 29.3 | 57.2 | 27.5 | 30.0 | 57.5 | 27.4 | 30.5 | 57.9 |

birth of the second child for four years spend the most. For example, focusing on the medium-income family, we find that an average of $81,300 is spent on each child if the interval between the two children is only one year. This average rises to $84,750 when the interval is increased to four years.

Children possess an economic advantage if they are separated by four years instead of one because each child spends a longer time in the parental household as the "only" child. Then, there is no sibling to compete for parental expenditures. On the other hand, parents can economize on child-related expenditures by spacing children closer together, though having several children in college simultaneously can impose heavy financial burdens on some families. Moreover, having children close together reduces the opportunity expenditure on children in families where the mother works by enabling the mother to spend less time out of the labor market and thereby reduce the foregone earnings attributable to children.

## Timing

One other assumption about the characteristics of families concerns the age of the wife at the time she bears her first child. For the preceding estimates, we assumed that the wife was age 25 and her husband was two years older when the first child was born. Recently in the United States a noticeable trend toward delaying childbearing has occurred and, consequently, substantial interest exists in the effects of this trend on the welfare of children and their families. We have included some additional estimates based on alternative assumptions regarding the age of the mother at the time her first child is born. New estimates of expenditures were computed for each child in a two-child family where the wife works part time, assuming that the wife is either 22, 27, or 32 when her first child is born. These particular ages were chosen to coincide with the age groups used in an Urban Institute study on delayed childbearing.[3]

Data from table 18 indicate that parents who delay the birth of their first child tend to spend more on their children. Results for an average child at the medium-income level show that parents can expect to spend $80,300 per child if the wife is age 22 when the first child is born, $82,800 if the wife is 27, and $83,200 if the wife waits until she is 32 years old. Although this pattern holds across each income level, only small increases in expenditures for both the medium and the low SES groups occur. Only in the high SES families does delayed childbearing make an appreciable difference in terms of subsequent expenditures on children.

One likely reason for the positive association between wife's age at first birth and the level of child-related expenditures is the upward slope to

TABLE 18   Parental Expenditures on Children by Wife's Age at First Birth, Total United States, 1981 Prices
(*Expenditures in thousands of dollars*)

| | | Wife's Employment Status: Part-time, Full-year Worker, Wife's Age at First Birth | | | | | | | | |
| | | 22 Years | | | 27 Years | | | 32 Years | | |
| Socioeconomic Status Group | Age Group | First Child | Second Child | Total | First Child | Second Child | Total | First Child | Second Child | Total |
|---|---|---|---|---|---|---|---|---|---|---|
| High | 0–17 | $95.3 | $92.7 | $188.0 | $102.1 | $97.8 | $199.9 | $104.7 | $100.6 | $205.4 |
| | 0–5 | 25.3 | 19.0 | 44.3 | 29.3 | 22.1 | 51.4 | 31.1 | 24.7 | 55.8 |
| | 6–11 | 33.6 | 35.2 | 68.7 | 35.4 | 36.7 | 72.0 | 36.5 | 37.3 | 73.8 |
| | 12–17 | 36.5 | 38.5 | 74.9 | 37.4 | 39.0 | 76.5 | 37.2 | 38.7 | 75.8 |
| Medium | 0–17 | 82.4 | 78.2 | 160.6 | 85.4 | 80.2 | 165.6 | 85.3 | 81.1 | 166.4 |
| | 0–5 | 22.8 | 16.1 | 38.9 | 25.2 | 17.8 | 43.0 | 25.6 | 19.6 | 45.2 |
| | 6–11 | 29.1 | 30.1 | 59.1 | 29.6 | 30.4 | 60.0 | 29.8 | 30.3 | 60.1 |
| | 12–17 | 30.5 | 32.1 | 62.6 | 30.7 | 32.0 | 62.6 | 29.9 | 31.2 | 61.1 |
| Low | 0–17 | 75.4 | 71.1 | 146.5 | 77.7 | 72.5 | 150.2 | 77.0 | 73.2 | 150.2 |
| | 0–5 | 20.9 | 14.2 | 35.1 | 22.9 | 15.7 | 38.6 | 23.0 | 17.4 | 40.4 |
| | 6–11 | 26.7 | 27.6 | 54.3 | 26.9 | 27.7 | 54.6 | 27.0 | 27.4 | 54.4 |
| | 12–17 | 27.8 | 29.3 | 57.1 | 27.9 | 29.1 | 57.0 | 27.1 | 28.3 | 55.4 |

the curve relating earnings to parents' age. Children who are born later in their parents' lives are being reared at a time when their parents have higher earnings. Consequently, family income is higher and more resources are available for child-related purchases. An explanation for the greater increase in expenditures in the higher SES families can be found in the shape of the earnings curve for husbands in white-collar jobs. The earnings of men at the high SES level are predicted to peak at age 49 in contrast to age 44 for men in blue-collar jobs. Consequently, children in low and medium SES families (where mothers are age 32 when they bear their first child) reach their most expensive years when their fathers' earnings have already peaked and are declining.

## Comparisons with Earlier Studies

Before the availability of data from the 1972–1973 Consumer Expenditure Survey (CES), the 1960–1961 Survey of Consumer Expenditures (SCE), also sponsored by the U.S. Bureau of Labor Statistics (BLS), was an important source for estimating parental expenditures on children. Therefore, examining the similarities and differences between our estimates and those derived from the 1960–1961 SCE is of interest.

Why might we expect our results to differ? For one thing, the level of overall prices increased by 44.9 percent between 1960–1961 and 1972–1973 so that estimates expressed in terms of the latter period would be higher than those from the former.[4] More importantly, however, real income grew by 45.5 percent between 1960 and 1973,[5] and this growth could have had an important effect in altering the pattern of consumer purchases between 1960–1961 and 1972–1973.

Evidence that consumers did indeed reallocate the way they spent their dollars over this period is contained in table 19. As table 19 shows, spending on every item increased between 1960–1961 and 1972–1973, but the rate of increase was more rapid for some items than for others. For example, the transportation share of total spending rose by more than 40 percent (from 15.2 percent of the total to 21.4 percent). This increase is largely attributable to expenditures connected with automobiles such as vehicle purchases, finance charges, maintenance costs, insurance, and gasoline. Associated with this rise was an increase in the average number of autos from 1.0 per family to 1.3 per family (Jacobs 1977). Housing costs also increased as a share of total expenditures (from 28.4 to 31.4 percent). Housing in 1972–1973 maintained its position from 1960–1961 as the most

TABLE 19    Consumption Expenditure Patterns, 1960-1961 and 1972-1973

| | 1960-1961 | | 1972-1973 | |
| Component | Average Expenditure | Percentage of Total | Average Expenditure | Percentage of Total |
|---|---|---|---|---|
| Total current consumption | $5,054 | 100.0 | $8,282 | 100.0 |
| Food, total | 1,234 | 24.4 | 1,664 | 20.1 |
| Food at home | 989 | 19.6 | 1,162 | 14.0 |
| Food away from home | 246 | 4.9 | 501 | 6.0 |
| Housing, total | 1,433 | 28.4 | 2,604 | 31.4 |
| Shelter | 664 | 13.1 | 1,362 | 16.4 |
| Utilities | 249 | 4.9 | 409 | 4.9 |
| Household operations | 253 | 5.0 | 447 | 5.4 |
| House furnishings | 266 | 5.3 | 387 | 4.7 |
| Clothing materials | 553 | 10.9 | 647 | 7.8 |
| Medical care | 340 | 6.7 | 528 | 6.4 |
| Transportation, total | 770 | 15.2 | 1,768 | 21.4 |
| Private transportation | 693 | 13.7 | 1,566 | 18.9 |
| Public and other | 77 | 1.5 | 201 | 2.4 |
| Miscellaneous, total | 723 | 14.3 | 1,072 | 12.9 |
| Recreation | 200 | 4.0 | 388 | 4.7 |
| Personal care | 145 | 2.9 | 165 | 2.0 |
| Education | 53 | 1.0 | 103 | 1.2 |
| Reading | 45 | 0.9 | 48 | 0.6 |
| Alcohol | 78 | 1.5 | 118 | 1.4 |
| Tobacco | 91 | 1.8 | 130 | 1.6 |
| Other miscellaneous | 111 | 2.2 | 120 | 1.5 |

SOURCE: Eva Jacobs (1977), table 1.

important category of consumption. Expenditures for total food, clothing, medical care, and miscellaneous items declined as a share of the total, although the percentage allocated to food away from home registered a small gain.

The rising importance of transportation expenditures can be seen in another way. In 1960-1961, transportation was third in importance, ranking behind housing and total food. But by the most recent survey, transportation had surpassed total food to stand second behind housing. In commenting on the trends, Jacobs (1977, p. 34) has remarked: "In general, the movements [in table 19] continue the direction of the changes in consumption patterns that occurred between the 1950s and 1960s. However, the increase in automobile transportation expenditures greatly exceeded the increase during the previous decade."

## Expenditure Estimates from the 1960–1961 and 1972–1973 Surveys

We shall limit our comparisons of estimates from the 1972–1973 CES to just two major investigations based on the 1960–1961 SCE: the study by Espenshade (1973) and the ongoing work by Carolyn Edwards (1981) at the U.S. Department of Agriculture (USDA). Espenshade's estimates have never been adjusted for inflation and are expressed in their original 1960–1961 price levels, whereas Edwards has issued yearly updates of estimates produced by the USDA in the 1960s.[6] Because they are expressed in terms of 1981 prices and therefore refer to the same period as our estimates from the 1972–1973 survey, data published by Edwards in the Winter 1982 issue of *Family Economics Review* serve as the basis for our discussion.[7] In examining the alternative estimates we shall mainly be interested in their implications for total expenditures to age 18, how these estimates vary by family income, family size, birth order of the child, age of child, and category of consumption, and what fraction of family income goes to children's consumption.

Our principal results comparing expenditures to age 18 on children in two-child families are contained in table 20. From the 1972–1973 CES we estimate that approximately $82,400 would be spent per child in a medium SES family. This figure is close to the USDA total of $80,400, averaged across all four census regions in moderate-cost urban families. The per child average for middle-income families in Espenshade's (1973) data is significantly lower at $30,721, but it has not been updated for inflation. An approximate adjustment is obtained by applying the increase of 205.4 percent in the overall CPI between 1960–1961 and 1981 to $30,721.[8] Doing so yields $93,834 in 1981 prices. However, this estimate includes as expenditures on children expenses for such things as insurance, gifts, and savings, and when these items are excluded to provide greater comparability with the USDA and 1972–1973 survey totals, the per child estimate is reduced to $74,628. On balance, when consideration is given to the underlying differences in estimation procedures, the three sources in table 20 yield estimates that appear to be not that far apart.

The data in table 20 also indicate quite clearly that parental expenditures on children increase with the level of family income. This finding accords with our intuition; when family income rises more resources are available to be spent on all family members. Child-related purchases in upper-income or high SES families tend to exceed by about 30 percent similar expenditures in lower-income or low SES families (the difference is

TABLE 20   Expenditures on Children to Age 18 by Birth Order and in Relation to Income in Two-child Families, 1960–1961 Survey of Consumer Expenditures (SCE) and 1972–1973 Consumer Expenditure Survey (CES)

| Item | 1960–1961 SCE | | | | 1972–1973 CES | | |
| --- | --- | --- | --- | --- | --- | --- | --- |
| | 1960–1961 Prices[a] | | | 1981 Prices[b] | 1981 Prices[c] | | |
| | Upper Income | Middle Income | Lower Income | Moderate Cost | High SES | Medium SES | Low SES |
| Total expenditure to age 18 | | | | | | | |
| First child | $47,045 | $41,119 | $37,655 | Ranges from $75,736 in North Central to $83,882 in West. Mean is $80,400. | $100,200 | $84,900 | $77,500 |
| Second child | 24,599 | 20,324 | 17,928 | | 96,400 | 80,000 | 72,500 |
| Both children | 71,644 | 61,442 | 55,583 | | 196,600 | 164,800 | 149,900 |
| Per child | 35,822 | 30,721 | 27,792 | | 98,300 | 82,400 | 74,950 |
| Ratio of second child to first child | 0.523 | 0.494 | 0.476 | NA[d] | 0.962 | 0.942 | 0.935 |
| Expenditure to age 18 as a percentage of income[e,f] | | | | | | | |
| First child | 24.6 | 30.5 | 38.5 | 21.5 | 13.4–24.0 | 17.3–23.9 | 20.1–23.8 |
| Second child | 12.5 | 14.7 | 17.9 | 21.5 | 12.2–22.1 | 15.8–21.7 | 18.5–21.5 |
| Both children | 33.4 | 40.7 | 50.8 | 43.0 | 23.2–41.3 | 29.9–40.7 | 34.8–40.4 |

a. Espenshade (1973), table 9. Income levels refer to projected streams of annual life-cycle after-tax family income, expressed in constant 1960–1961 dollars. Annual income at the upper level ranges between $9,007 and $11,698; at the middle level between $6,326 and $8,120; and at the lower level between $4,564 and $5,879.

b. U.S. Department of Agriculture (1982), based on expenditures on an average child in urban United States, in a husband-wife family with no more than five children, spending at the moderate cost level.

c. Table 3, assumes mothers working part time.

d. Not applicable. USDA estimates are for an average child in a family and are not derived separately for each birth order.

e. Calculated as a percentage of income in the appropriate 18-year period (or 20 years in the case of both children combined).

f. The definition of income in these studies is as follows: Espenshade (1973) uses after-tax family income. The USDA estimates are calculated as a percentage of average annual disposable family income (see U.S. Department of Agriculture, 1971, table 6). USDA figures shown in the table for expenditures on children as a percentage of income are based on an average of moderate-cost two-child families in the North Central and South census regions. If family size is ignored, expenditure per child ranges between about 15 and 17 percent of disposable income. For estimates calculated from the 1972–1973 CES, a range is provided. The lower figure in each instance uses estimated before-tax family income in the denominator, whereas the higher figure is calculated as a percentage of estimated total family current consumption expenditures. An estimate of child-related expenditures as a percentage of after-tax or disposable family income would fall somewhere between these limits.

28.9 percent in the 1960–1961 survey and 31.2 percent in the 1972–1973 data). Differences also seem associated with the birth order of the child in the family. Data from the 1960–1961 SCE imply that only half as much is spent on the younger child as on the older child in two-child families, though this ratio may be too low (Espenshade 1973). The 1972–1973 CES suggests, on the other hand, that economies of scale in rearing second children may not exceed 6 or 7 percent of expenditures on the first child.

Because the estimates of child-related parental expenditures that persons encounter in the media are constantly shifting owing to, among other things, rising prices, it is perhaps of greater interest to know what fraction of its income a couple is likely to devote to child-rearing expenditures. The bottom portion of table 20 contains information on this important topic. We can calculate this proportion in our 1972–1973 estimates in two ways: (1) in relation to projected total family income (before taxes) or (2) in relation to estimated total family current consumption. Since the numerator will be the same in either case (estimated expenditures on children), the percentage we compute will be smaller using before-tax family income in the denominator than total current consumption.

For the 1972–1973 data in table 20, the range we give reflects the use of these alternative denominators. The upper limits on this range vary hardly at all with changes in socioeconomic status, suggesting that approximately 40 percent of total family current consumption is attributable to children's consumption in two-child families. On the other hand, the percentage of before-tax family income devoted to child-bearing expenses goes down as family income increases—from about 35 percent in low SES families to about 23 percent in high SES families. This declining proportion as family income rises reflects, among other things, the proportionately higher taxes paid by higher-income groups. Data from the 1960–1961 SCE rely on disposable (or after-tax) family income in the denominator. Both Espenshade's (1973) and the USDA's (1982) estimates indicate that, in average-income two-child families, roughly 40–45 percent of disposable family income is allocated to children.

Differences between 1960–1961 and 1972–1973 survey estimates of child-related purchases according to the child's age are shown in table 21. A noticeable similarity occurs in the age estimates derived from the 1972–1973 CES and by the USDA, whereas Espenshade's (1973) distribution is more heavily skewed toward ages 12–17.

Based on the evidence in table 19 of a marked shift in spending patterns between 1960–1961 and 1972–1973, we might expect estimates of expenditures on children derived from these two periods to exhibit the greatest differences when they are disaggregated by category of consumption.

TABLE 21     Age Distribution of Parental Expenditures on Children in Two-child
             Families, 1960-1961 SCE and 1972-1973 CES

|  | 1960-1961 SCE | | | | 1972-1973 CES | |
|  | 1960-1961 Prices[a] | | 1981 Prices[b] | | 1981 Prices[c] | |
| Age Group | Dollars | Percentage | Dollars | Percentage | Dollars | Percentage |
|---|---|---|---|---|---|---|
| First Child |  |  |  |  |  |  |
| 0-5 | $ 5,980 | 14.4 | $22,839 | 28.6 | $24,700 | 29.1 |
| 6-11 | 13,853 | 33.7 | 26,432 | 33.1 | 29,400 | 34.6 |
| 12-17 | 21,358 | 51.9 | 30,637 | 38.3 | 30,700 | 36.2 |
| Total | 41,119 | 100.0 | 79,908 | 100.0 | 84,900 | 100.0 |
| Second Child |  |  |  |  |  |  |
| 0-5 | 1,977 | 9.7 | 22,839 | 28.6 | 17,500 | 21.9 |
| 6-11 | 5,037 | 24.8 | 26,432 | 33.1 | 30,300 | 37.9 |
| 12-17 | 13,310 | 65.5 | 30,637 | 38.3 | 32,200 | 40.3 |
| Total | 20,324 | 100.0 | 79,908 | 100.0 | 80,000 | 100.0 |

a. Espenshade (1973), table 10, middle-income level, two-child families.

b. U.S. Department of Agriculture (1982), based on expenditures on an average child in the urban Northeast, in a husband-wife family with no more than five children, spending at the moderate cost level.

c. Table 3, medium SES, two-child families, mothers working part time.

The data in table 22 highlight our findings. Beginning on the left-hand side of this table, we see that in 1960-1961 food ranked first in importance among all categories of expenditure on first children in two-child families, composing one-quarter (25.4 percent) of total expenditures to age 18. Housing was in second place (20.2 percent), followed at some distance by clothing (14.4 percent) and miscellaneous other expenditures (13.2 percent). For second children, food expenditures again led the list, taking up a quarter of the total (25.3 percent). But whereas net saving was a relatively trivial component of expense for first children, this category jumped to second place (18.0 percent) for the second child.[9] Following net saving in third and fourth position were housing (16.0 percent) and clothing expenditures (11.5 percent), respectively. We may conclude that in 1960-1961, food dominated all other purchases in the child's total budget, comprising one-quarter of all expenses, and that, apart from net saving, housing and clothing came in second and third place.

Both the USDA and the 1972-1973 CES estimates in table 22 have been updated to 1981 by taking figures expressed initially in either 1960-1961 or 1972-1973 price levels and applying the appropriate category-

TABLE 22  Parental Expenditures on Children in Two-child Families by Category of Expenditure, 1960–1961 SCE and 1972–1973 CES

| | 1960–1961 SCE | | | | 1972–1973 CES | |
|---|---|---|---|---|---|---|
| | *1960–1961 Prices[a]* | | *1981 Prices[b]* | | *1981 Prices[c]* | |
| *Components of Total Expenditure to Age 18* | *Dollars* | *Percentage* | *Dollars* | *Percentage* | *Dollars* | *Percentage* |
| First Child | | | | | | |
| Food, total | $10,432 | 25.4 | $20,886 | 26.1 | $19,000 | 22.4 |
| Food at home | | | 18,830 | 23.6 | 15,100 | 17.8 |
| Food away from home | | | 2,056 | 2.6 | 3,900 | 4.6 |
| Housing, total | 8,320 | 20.2 | 27,302 | 34.2 | 19,700 | 23.2 |
| Shelter | | | | | 6,900 | 8.1 |
| Fuel and utilities | | | | | 4,000 | 4.7 |
| Household goods and operations | | | | | 8,800 | 10.4 |
| Clothing | 5,937 | 14.4 | 5,888 | 7.4 | 6,300 | 7.4 |
| Transportation | 1,422 | 3.5 | 11,864 | 14.8 | 21,800 | 25.7 |
| Medical care | 2,694 | 6.6 | 3,942 | 4.9 | 4,800 | 5.7 |
| Recreation | | | | | 8,300 | 9.8 |
| Education | | | 1,368 | 1.7 | | |
| Other | 5,443[d] | 13.2 | 8,658[e] | 10.8 | 4,900[f] | 5.8 |
| Insurance | 3,274 | 8.0 | | | | |
| Gifts | 1,932 | 4.7 | | | | |
| Net saving | 1,665 | 4.1 | | | | |
| Total | 41,119 | 100.0 | 79,908 | 100.0 | 84,900 | 100.0 |
| Second Child | | | | | | |
| Food, total | $ 5,146 | 25.3 | $20,886 | 26.1 | $18,100 | 22.6 |
| Food at home | | | 18,830 | 23.6 | 14,600 | 18.3 |
| Food away from home | | | 2,056 | 2.6 | 3,500 | 4.4 |
| Housing, total | 3,260 | 16.0 | 27,302 | 34.2 | 20,000 | 25.0 |
| Shelter | | | | | 8,100 | 10.1 |
| Fuel and utilities | | | | | 3,800 | 4.8 |
| Household goods and operations | | | | | 8,100 | 10.1 |
| Clothing | 2,343 | 11.5 | 5,888 | 7.4 | 5,800 | 7.3 |
| Transportation | 1,191 | 5.9 | 11,864 | 14.8 | 19,600 | 24.5 |
| Medical care | 715 | 3.5 | 3,942 | 4.9 | 4,600 | 5.8 |
| Recreation | | | | | 7,500 | 9.4 |
| Education | | | 1,368 | 1.7 | | |
| Other | 1,964[d] | 9.7 | 8,658[e] | 10.8 | 4,400[f] | 5.5 |
| Insurance | 1,254 | 6.2 | | | | |
| Gifts | 801 | 3.9 | | | | |
| Net saving | 3,651 | 18.0 | | | | |
| Total | 20,324 | 100.0 | 79,908 | 100.0 | 80,000 | 100.0 |

a. Espenshade (1973), table 12, middle-income, two-child families.

b. U.S. Department of Agriculture (1982), based on expenditures on an average child in the urban Northeast region, in a husband-wife family with no more than five children, spending at the moderate cost level.

c. Table 4.14, medium SES, two-child families, mothers working part time.

d. Includes personal care, recreation, reading, education and miscellaneous expenditures.

e. Includes personal care, recreation, reading and other miscellaneous expenditures.

f. Includes alcohol, tobacco, personal care, reading, education, and miscellaneous expenditures.

specific rates of inflation up to 1981. The primary differences between these two sets of estimates therefore reflect the combined effects of (1) differences in underlying estimation procedures and (2) the use in the case of the USDA figures of an older set of income and consumption data. The USDA estimates show housing to be the most important item in the child's budget, constituting over one-third (34.2 percent) of total expenditures to age 18. Food is next in importance at 26.1 percent (most of this is accounted for by food at home), followed by transportation at 14.8 percent. When combined, housing, food, and transportation make up three-quarters (75.1 percent) of all expenditures on children, according to USDA calculations.

Data from the 1972–1973 CES reveal a different pattern of expenditures on children. When housing, food, and transportation purchases for children are combined, they again reach nearly three-quarters of all expenditures on children (71.3 percent for the first child and 72.1 percent for second children), but the individual components are much more nearly equal than they are in the USDA estimates, and the relative ranking of each commodity group in the 1972–1973 estimates depends on the birth order of the child. Transportation leads the list for first births (25.7 percent), followed by housing (23.2 percent), whereas for second births housing (25.0 percent) is slightly more important than is transportation (24.5 percent). For either birth order, food consumption comes in third place.

A primary difference between the USDA and the 1972–1973 CES estimates appears to be with the pattern of expenditures on children by category of consumption and not so much with the overall level of expenditures. The USDA estimates attribute more importance to food at home and less to food away from home and to transportation than figures derived from the 1972–1973 CES. But as we saw in table 19, this is the kind of result expected when relying on 1960–1961 expenditure patterns. At the same time, the 1972–1973 CES estimates of housing expenditures for children are proportionately smaller than the USDA estimates are, despite an increase in the relative share of housing in the market basket of all consumers between 1960–1961 and 1972–1973. This anomaly derives from basic differences between the way we and the USDA conceptualize and measure parental expenditures on children. As we shall see in more detail in the following pages, the USDA approach is to estimate expenditure on the *average* child, whereas our method focuses on expenditures on the *additional* (or marginal) child.

How are expenditures on children affected by variations in family size, region of the country, or residence in an urban or rural area? In the last part of this chapter we compare results on these questions based on the 1960–1961 SCE with those obtained from the 1972–1973 CES. First, with regard to family size, our data from the 1972–1973 CES showed that expenditures per child declined significantly with increases in the number of children, other things held constant. If we recall our previous example of a medium SES family where the wife works part time, expenditures per child fell from $106,200 to $82,400 when family size increased from one to two children, and they fell further to $68,800 when three children were present. Comparing one- and three-child families, we find that expenditures per child are 35 percent smaller in the latter case than in the former. If we now examine middle-income families in Espenshade's (1973) analysis of the 1960–1961 SCE data, we find that expenditures per child to age 18 decline from $42,565 in one-child families to $30,721 in two-child families to $26,369 in three-child families. The decline of $16,196 per child that accompanies the transition from one to three children per family represents a 38 percent drop, a figure which is very close to our 1972–1973 CES estimate.[10]

To repeat our conclusions on the regional variations in child-related purchases, we found that parents in the Northeast and in the West generally devoted larger sums to their children's upbringing than did parents in the North Central and South regions. In families where mothers were not employed, children had the most spent on them in the West and the least in the South. Data for 1981 from the USDA (1982) show that, for urban children, expenditures per child at the moderate-cost level range from a high of $83,882 in the West to a low of $75,736 in the North Central region. For rural nonfarm children, the West is again the most expensive region at $87,491 per child, and this figure declines to a low of $70,639 in the North Central region. In the USDA data, the South ranks as second most expensive behind the West in the urban children sample and third most expensive in the rural nonfarm sample.

Finally, we may compare our metropolitan-nonmetropolitan estimates with the urban-rural nonfarm data from the USDA (1982). In our data, families living in metropolitan areas (inside SMSAs) consistently outspend families in nonmetropolitan areas (outside SMSAs) in rearing their children. According to our calculations, a two-child family at the medium SES level with a wife working full time spends $98,700 per child to age 18 if the family resides in a metropolitan area versus $83,500 per child in nonmetropolitan areas. The metropolitan total is 18.2 percent higher than the nonmetropolitan one. USDA figures indicate that, in three out of four census regions, parents in rural nonfarm areas spend more on their children than parents do in urban ones. Only in the North Central region is the urban child more expensive than the rural nonfarm one ($75,736 vs. $70,639). If we take a simple average across all census regions, then rural nonfarm children appear to have more spent on them than urban children do ($81,565 vs. $80,400). This conclusion contradicts our findings from the 1972–1973 CES.

## Commentary on the USDA Estimates

Because the estimates we have derived from the 1972–1973 CES bear a greater resemblance to the USDA estimates than to Espenshade's (1973) figures, it is worth examining some of the similarities and differences between the USDA procedures and ours. In many respects the aims of the two studies are the same; both are concerned with estimating how much parents actually spend in direct out-of-pocket purchases to rear their children to age 18, and not with how much children "cost" or with how much is required for their upbringing. Moreover, both studies illustrate the variations in child-related expenditures associated with differences in the age of the child, family economic position, region of the country, place of residence, and category of consumption.

At the same time, the individual studies possess distinctive features, characterized by the choice of data sets and by the estimation procedures employed. To repeat, the Department of Agriculture numbers are derived from the 1960–1961 SCE, whereas ours are based on the 1972–1973 CES. But beyond the data, important methodological differences appear.[11]

Three important differences occur in the methods of estimation. The first concerns how standard of living is incorporated into the analysis. In our work, estimates are provided for three different socioeconomic status groups in the population: high, medium, and low. These SES categories are determined on the basis of some relatively fixed background characteristics, principally, the education and occupation of the household head. Our methods assume that the head's education and occupation are held constant over the life cycle, although family income may vary in response to changes in the husband's age or in the wife's age and/or employment status. When coupled with the fact that children are entering the household, aging, and eventually leaving home, our methods permit the family's material standard of living to be endogenous and thus to vary over the life cycle.

By contrast, the USDA estimates are calculated for each of several "cost levels." Estimates of the expenditures on urban and rural nonfarm children are produced for economy-, low-, and moderate-cost levels. Four cost levels are used for farm children—thrifty (similar to economy), low, moderate, and liberal. These cost levels reflect spending patterns connected with food consumption at the levels of the USDA food plans. According to Edwards (1981, 10), "The estimates were developed holding the cost level constant. In other words, the estimates do not reflect changes in income or level of living typically experienced by families as their children age." This is an important limitation of the USDA approach because their basic assumption that a family's level of living remains constant over the time that children are in the home is contradicted by other evidence. For example, in earlier work, Espenshade (1973, 78–79) concluded, "A family's standard of living, measured in terms of current consumption, declines (although real income is allowed to increase) until the eldest child reaches age eighteen, then starts to rise again. This decline is steeper and more prolonged the greater the number of children." Data from our current study tell a similar story. In medium SES, two-child families in which the mother works part time, the percentage of total family current consumption allocated to food at home (an indicator that, we postulate, varies inversely with a family's material standard of living) rises from 11.4 in the first year of the elder child's life to a maximum of 19.0 when the two children are 10 and 8 years old, and then falls gradually to 17.1 when the children are 17 and 15 years old. Therefore consistent evidence points out that family living standards do indeed change over the life cycle, and that the change is usually in a negative direction during much of the time children are in the household.[12]

A second methodological difference between the two studies is that our figures reflect marginal expenditures whereas those from the USDA show average expenditures per child. By marginal expenditures, we mean that we distribute total expenditures on children in a family into birth-order-specific estimates (that is, separately for the first child, for the second, and so on). In the USDA approach, total expenditures on children are divided by the number of children to produce a per child average. Our estimates of marginal expenditures can easily be converted to a per child average, but whether the USDA data can be transformed into marginal expenditure estimates is unclear.[13]

USDA figures are average expenditure estimates because their methodology relies on a *per capita share* approach. That is, family costs are frequently allocated on a per capita (or pro rata) basis to individual family members. This per capita share method forces an average expenditure interpretation on the results. This technique was used exclusively to estimate expenditures on children for housing, transportation, and miscellaneous other items. And it was used with other procedures in estimating expenditures on food away from home, clothing, medical care, and education. The use of a per capita share method to derive housing expenditures attributable to children helps to explain why the USDA estimate for housing is proportionately larger than ours. In a two-child family, one-fourth of family housing costs would be assigned to each child with the USDA method, whereas using our approach, only the *extra* housing expenditures needed to maintain the same standard of living would be allocated to children. Since the housing that a childless couple would purchase would likely contain some minimal number of rooms, and the number of extra bedrooms is the main variable housing cost associated with children, our estimation procedure would ordinarily allocate less than one-fourth of family housing expenditures to each child in a two-child family.

A third factor distinguishing our work from that of the USDA is that our estimates explicitly take the wife's employment status into account. Commenting on the sample of husband-wife households analyzed in the 1960–1961 SCE, Edwards (1981, 32) says, "It is probably reasonable to assume that most of these nuclear families were also single-earner families." One may ask then how relevant the USDA results are to today's circumstances when labor force participation rates for married women exceed 50 percent.[14] Edwards adds, "Families of differing structure are likely to have different spending patterns, which may affect total costs as well as costs for specific categories. For example, expenses for transportation are affected by the number of full-time earners employed outside the home" (p. 32). But Edwards does not provide any explicit instructions on how to adjust for wife's employment status.

## Projections for Children Born in 1981

The estimates described up to now assume the continuation of 1981 price levels throughout the period parents are making expenditures on their children. But the assumption of stable prices is not a tenable one, especially in light of recent U.S. experience. Therefore, it is of interest to know how much larger our estimates would be if we took probable future inflation rates into account.

Our estimates will assume that couples have their first child in 1981. If they have a total of three children spaced two years apart, then subsequent births will occur in 1983 and in 1985. In addition, we will build our estimates around three future inflation scenarios. The low inflation series assumes that the future annual inflation rate for each of our ten categories of consumption will equal the annual average inflation rate for the particular commodity group when the average is taken over the twenty-two years between June 1959 and June 1981. The use of a twenty-two year time span is not wholly arbitrary; it corresponds to the approximate age when many young people graduate from college. The medium inflation series is derived in a similar manner by projecting the average annual inflation rates for each category of consumption, when averaged over the ten years separating June 1971 and June 1981. The average annual experience for the five years between June 1976 and June 1981 is used for the high inflation series.

Table 23 contains the actual inflation rates used in the projections. In general, the low inflation scenario assumes an annual inflation rate of 5.2 percent (when based on all items); the medium series corresponds to 8.0

TABLE 23   Assumed Inflation Rates for Projecting Post-1981 Expenditures on Children; Low, Medium, and High Inflation Series

| | Average Annual Inflation Rate (Percentage) | | |
|---|---|---|---|
| *Item* | *Low[a]* | *Medium[a]* | *High[a]* |
| Food at home | 5.007 | 8.280 | 8.046 |
| Food away from home | 5.909 | 8.365 | 8.967 |
| Shelter | 5.877 | 8.906 | 11.240 |
| Fuel and utilities | 5.615 | 10.275 | 11.332 |
| Household goods | 5.675[b] | 6.433 | 6.456 |
| Clothing | 3.407 | 4.363 | 4.698 |
| Transportation | 5.193 | 8.503 | 10.461 |
| Health care | 6.099 | 8.183 | 9.235 |
| Recreation | 5.679[b] | 5.826 | 6.454 |
| Miscellaneous | 6.112[b] | 6.520 | 7.303 |
| All items | 5.154 | 8.033 | 9.337 |

a. The low series assumes a continuation of average annual inflation rates between June 1959 and June 1981. The middle series is based on the period June 1971 to June 1981, and the high series includes June 1976 to June 1981.

b. Based on 14 years' experience, from June 1967 to June 1981.

percent annual inflation; and the high series assumes 9.3 percent annual inflation.

The procedures used for producing the projections described in this section are as follows. We begin with our estimates of total expenditures on each child, expressed in 1981 prices and disaggregated by single years of the child's age and by category of expenditure. For each age ($x$) of each child we first ascertain the calendar year (YR) the child will be that age. For instance, the eldest child in our examples will be under age 1 in 1981, age 1 in 1982, and so forth. Then, for each one of our ten categories of expenditure, we compute the projected price inflation between 1981 and YR and multiply it by the estimated expenditure (in 1981 prices) on that item when the child is age $x$. This procedure is repeated for each age $x$ and for each child. Adding across the inflation-adjusted expenditure categories at age $x$ produces the inflation-adjusted total for that age.

Tables 24, 25, and 26 contain estimates of parental expenditures on children when the eldest child is born in 1981, under three different inflation scenarios. Estimates of expenditures are broken down by level of family income, family size, age of child, and wife's employment status. Total expenditures on children depend importantly on the particular assumption about future inflation. For example, consider again the two-child medium-income family where the wife is employed part time. Under the low inflation scenario, our estimates indicate that $149,150 will be the average expenditure per child up to age 18. A total of $199,650 is predicted for the same child under the medium inflation scenario, and $227,700 is the estimated total with the high inflation assumption. In tables 24, 25, and 26 higher birth order children appear more expensive because they are being reared at a time when projected average price levels are at their highest.

The reader will recall that the estimate for the same child was $82,400 in 1981 prices. If high inflation rates continued to be the norm over the next two decades, our inflation-adjusted total estimate of $227,700 would be nearly three times the 1981 estimate. It is important to note, however, that it is not only expenditures that will be affected by inflation. Parents' income will also be expected to grow, and there is no basis for thinking, other things the same, that children's consumption will comprise a larger fraction of total family consumption in the future than it does now.

The estimates presented in tables 24, 25, and 26 do not include any projections for future college costs. The expenses of four years of college are substantial, and many parents would want to include these costs in their estimates. The Oakland Financial Group projected college costs for a child born about 1976.[15] Although these figures are likely to be conserva-

TABLE 24 Estimated Future Parental Expenditures on Children When the First Child Is Born in 1981, Low Inflation Scenario (*Expenditures in thousands of dollars*)

| Socioeconomic Status Group | Age Group | One-child Families Total | Wife's Employment Status: Full-time, Full-year Worker | | | | | | |
| | | | Two-child Families | | | Three-child Families | | | |
| | | | First Child | Second Child | Total | First Child | Second Child | Third Child | Total |
|---|---|---|---|---|---|---|---|---|---|
| High | 0–17 | $232.3 | $181.2 | $199.1 | $380.3 | $153.7 | $164.5 | $183.4 | $501.6 |
| | 0–5 | 42.4 | 37.3 | 32.3 | 69.6 | 37.7 | 30.0 | 24.9 | 92.6 |
| | 6–11 | 78.5 | 59.0 | 67.8 | 126.8 | 47.9 | 54.3 | 62.9 | 165.1 |
| | 12–17 | 111.4 | 84.9 | 99.0 | 183.9 | 68.1 | 80.2 | 95.6 | 243.9 |
| Medium | 0–17 | 207.3 | 162.4 | 176.8 | 339.2 | 138.2 | 146.6 | 162.6 | 447.4 |
| | 0–5 | 38.6 | 34.2 | 28.6 | 62.8 | 34.8 | 26.8 | 21.4 | 82.9 |
| | 6–11 | 70.5 | 53.0 | 60.6 | 113.6 | 43.1 | 48.6 | 56.1 | 147.8 |
| | 12–17 | 98.2 | 75.2 | 87.6 | 162.7 | 60.4 | 71.2 | 85.1 | 216.7 |
| Low | 0–17 | 195.2 | 153.3 | 166.3 | 319.6 | 130.7 | 138.2 | 153.0 | 421.9 |
| | 0–5 | 36.5 | 32.4 | 26.7 | 59.2 | 33.1 | 25.1 | 19.6 | 77.8 |
| | 6–11 | 66.6 | 50.1 | 57.2 | 107.3 | 40.8 | 45.9 | 53.0 | 139.6 |
| | 12–17 | 92.2 | 70.7 | 82.4 | 153.1 | 56.9 | 67.2 | 80.5 | 204.5 |

TABLE 24 (continued)  Estimated Future Parental Expenditures on Children When the First Child Is Born in 1981, Low Inflation Scenario
(Expenditures in thousands of dollars)

| Socioeconomic Status Group | Age Group | One-child Families Total | Wife's Employment Status: Part-time, Full-year Worker | | | | | | | |
| | | | Two-child Families | | | Three-child Families | | | |
| | | | First Child | Second Child | Total | First Child | Second Child | Third Child | Total |
|---|---|---|---|---|---|---|---|---|---|
| High | 0-17 | $217.6 | $169.9 | $188.0 | $357.9 | $144.0 | $155.4 | $174.5 | $474.0 |
| | 0-5 | 37.8 | 33.4 | 28.8 | 62.3 | 34.0 | 26.9 | 22.2 | 83.2 |
| | 6-11 | 73.4 | 55.2 | 64.0 | 119.3 | 44.8 | 51.3 | 59.9 | 156.1 |
| | 12-17 | 106.4 | 81.2 | 95.2 | 176.3 | 65.1 | 77.2 | 92.4 | 234.7 |
| Medium | 0-17 | 181.6 | 142.7 | 155.6 | 298.3 | 121.8 | 129.4 | 144.0 | 395.2 |
| | 0-5 | 32.7 | 29.3 | 23.9 | 53.1 | 30.0 | 22.6 | 17.4 | 70.1 |
| | 6-11 | 62.0 | 46.7 | 53.6 | 100.3 | 38.0 | 43.0 | 49.9 | 131.0 |
| | 12-17 | 86.9 | 66.8 | 78.1 | 144.9 | 53.8 | 63.8 | 76.6 | 194.2 |
| Low | 0-17 | 164.8 | 130.0 | 141.1 | 271.2 | 111.3 | 117.7 | 131.0 | 360.0 |
| | 0-5 | 29.8 | 26.8 | 21.3 | 48.1 | 27.7 | 20.3 | 15.1 | 63.1 |
| | 6-11 | 56.5 | 42.6 | 48.8 | 91.4 | 34.7 | 39.2 | 45.5 | 119.5 |
| | 12-17 | 78.5 | 60.6 | 71.1 | 131.7 | 48.9 | 58.2 | 70.3 | 117.5 |

TABLE 24  Estimated Future Parental Expenditures on Children When the First Child Is Born in 1981, Low Inflation Scenario
(*continued*) (*Expenditures in thousands of dollars*)

|  |  |  | Wife's Employment Status: Not Employed | | | | | | | |
|  |  | One-child Families | Two-child Families | | | Three-child Families | | | |
| Socioeconomic Status Group | Age Group | Total | First Child | Second Child | Total | First Child | Second Child | Third Child | Total |
|---|---|---|---|---|---|---|---|---|---|
| High | 0–17 | $204.0 | $159.4 | $177.4 | $336.8 | $135.1 | $146.8 | $165.8 | $447.7 |
|  | 0–5 | 34.0 | 30.2 | 25.9 | 56.1 | 30.9 | 24.3 | 19.9 | 75.2 |
|  | 6–11 | 68.8 | 51.8 | 60.5 | 112.2 | 42.1 | 48.5 | 57.0 | 147.5 |
|  | 12–17 | 101.3 | 77.4 | 91.1 | 168.5 | 62.2 | 74.0 | 88.8 | 225.0 |
| Medium | 0–17 | 168.2 | 132.5 | 144.4 | 277.0 | 113.3 | 120.3 | 134.1 | 367.7 |
|  | 0–5 | 29.9 | 26.9 | 21.6 | 48.4 | 27.7 | 20.5 | 15.5 | 63.8 |
|  | 6–11 | 57.6 | 43.4 | 49.9 | 93.4 | 35.4 | 40.1 | 46.7 | 122.2 |
|  | 12–17 | 80.7 | 62.2 | 72.9 | 135.2 | 50.2 | 59.7 | 71.9 | 181.8 |
| Low | 0–17 | 153.0 | 121.0 | 131.3 | 252.3 | 103.8 | 109.7 | 122.3 | 335.8 |
|  | 0–5 | 27.2 | 24.7 | 19.2 | 43.9 | 25.6 | 18.4 | 13.4 | 57.5 |
|  | 6–11 | 52.6 | 39.7 | 45.6 | 85.2 | 32.4 | 36.6 | 42.6 | 111.6 |
|  | 12–17 | 73.2 | 56.6 | 66.6 | 123.2 | 45.8 | 54.7 | 66.3 | 166.7 |

Note: This scenario assumes a continuation beyond 1981 of average annual inflation rates over the past 22 years.

TABLE 25   Estimated Future Parental Expenditures on Children When the First Child Is Born in 1981, Medium Inflation Scenario (Expenditures in thousands of dollars)

| Socioeconomic Status Group | Age Group | One-child Families Total | Two-child Families | | | Three-child Families | | | |
|---|---|---|---|---|---|---|---|---|---|
| | | | First Child | Second Child | Total | First Child | Second Child | Third Child | Total |
| High | 0–17 | $301.0 | $233.8 | $273.8 | $507.7 | $196.7 | $225.6 | $268.7 | $691.0 |
| | 0–5 | 45.8 | 40.1 | 36.9 | 77.0 | 40.6 | 34.1 | 30.3 | 105.0 |
| | 6–11 | 96.4 | 72.5 | 87.7 | 160.2 | 58.8 | 70.4 | 85.9 | 215.1 |
| | 12–17 | 158.7 | 121.2 | 149.2 | 270.4 | 97.3 | 121.1 | 152.5 | 371.0 |
| Medium | 0–17 | 268.2 | 209.4 | 243.2 | 452.6 | 176.9 | 201.2 | 238.6 | 616.7 |
| | 0–5 | 41.7 | 36.8 | 32.8 | 69.6 | 37.4 | 30.6 | 26.2 | 94.1 |
| | 6–11 | 86.6 | 65.2 | 78.4 | 143.6 | 53.0 | 63.0 | 76.6 | 192.6 |
| | 12–17 | 139.9 | 107.4 | 132.0 | 239.4 | 86.5 | 107.6 | 135.8 | 329.9 |
| Low | 0–17 | 252.6 | 197.6 | 229.0 | 426.6 | 167.3 | 189.8 | 225.0 | 582.0 |
| | 0–5 | 39.4 | 34.9 | 30.6 | 65.5 | 35.6 | 28.7 | 24.1 | 88.4 |
| | 6–11 | 81.8 | 61.6 | 74.0 | 135.6 | 50.1 | 59.5 | 72.3 | 182.0 |
| | 12–17 | 131.4 | 101.1 | 124.4 | 225.5 | 81.5 | 101.6 | 128.5 | 311.7 |

*Wife's Employment Status: Full-time, Full-year Worker*

TABLE 25 Estimated Future Parental Expenditures on Children When the First Child Is Born in 1981, Medium Inflation Scenario
(continued) (Expenditures in thousands of dollars)

| Socioeconomic Status Group | Age Group | One-child Families Total | Wife's Employment Status: Part-time, Full-year Worker | | | | | | |
|---|---|---|---|---|---|---|---|---|---|
| | | | Two-child Families | | | Three-child Families | | | |
| | | | First Child | Second Child | Total | First Child | Second Child | Third Child | Total |
| High | 0-17 | $282.7 | $219.9 | $259.4 | $479.3 | $185.0 | $213.8 | $256.4 | $655.3 |
| | 0-5 | 40.9 | 36.0 | 33.0 | 69.0 | 36.6 | 30.7 | 27.2 | 94.6 |
| | 6-11 | 90.3 | 67.9 | 82.9 | 150.8 | 55.2 | 66.5 | 81.8 | 203.5 |
| | 12-17 | 151.6 | 115.9 | 143.5 | 259.4 | 93.2 | 116.6 | 147.4 | 357.2 |
| Medium | 0-17 | 235.4 | 184.5 | 214.8 | 399.3 | 156.3 | 178.3 | 212.3 | 546.9 |
| | 0-5 | 35.4 | 31.5 | 27.4 | 59.0 | 32.4 | 25.9 | 21.5 | 79.8 |
| | 6-11 | 76.2 | 57.5 | 69.4 | 126.9 | 46.8 | 55.8 | 68.3 | 170.9 |
| | 12-17 | 123.9 | 95.5 | 117.9 | 213.4 | 77.2 | 96.6 | 122.5 | 296.2 |
| Low | 0-17 | 213.8 | 168.2 | 195.2 | 363.4 | 143.0 | 162.5 | 193.6 | 499.1 |
| | 0-5 | 32.2 | 28.9 | 24.5 | 53.4 | 29.9 | 23.3 | 18.8 | 71.9 |
| | 6-11 | 69.5 | 52.5 | 63.3 | 115.7 | 42.8 | 50.9 | 62.3 | 156.0 |
| | 12-17 | 112.1 | 86.8 | 107.4 | 194.2 | 70.3 | 88.3 | 112.5 | 271.2 |

TABLE 25   Estimated Future Parental Expenditures on Children When the First Child Is Born in 1981, Medium Inflation Scenario
(continued)   (Expenditures in thousands of dollars)

| Socioeconomic Status Group | Age Group | One-child Families | Wife's Employment Status: Not Employed | | | | | | |
|---|---|---|---|---|---|---|---|---|---|
| | | | Two-child Families | | | Three-child Families | | | |
| | | Total | First Child | Second Child | Total | First Child | Second Child | Third Child | Total |
| High | 0–17 | $265.7 | $206.9 | $245.4 | $452.3 | $174.1 | $202.5 | $244.1 | $620.8 |
| | 0–5 | 36.8 | 32.6 | 29.7 | 62.3 | 33.3 | 27.8 | 24.5 | 85.7 |
| | 6–11 | 84.6 | 63.7 | 78.3 | 142.0 | 51.8 | 62.9 | 77.8 | 192.5 |
| | 12–17 | 144.4 | 110.6 | 137.4 | 248.0 | 89.0 | 111.8 | 141.8 | 342.6 |
| Medium | 0–17 | 218.4 | 171.6 | 199.7 | 371.3 | 145.7 | 166.1 | 198.1 | 510.0 |
| | 0–5 | 32.3 | 29.0 | 24.8 | 53.8 | 29.9 | 23.5 | 19.3 | 72.7 |
| | 6–11 | 70.8 | 53.5 | 64.7 | 118.2 | 43.6 | 52.1 | 63.8 | 159.5 |
| | 12–17 | 115.2 | 89.1 | 110.2 | 199.3 | 72.1 | 90.5 | 115.1 | 277.7 |
| Low | 0–17 | 198.7 | 156.7 | 182.0 | 338.7 | 133.5 | 151.9 | 181.4 | 466.8 |
| | 0–5 | 29.5 | 26.6 | 22.2 | 48.8 | 27.7 | 21.2 | 16.8 | 65.7 |
| | 6–11 | 64.7 | 48.9 | 59.1 | 108.0 | 39.9 | 47.6 | 58.4 | 145.9 |
| | 12–17 | 104.5 | 81.2 | 100.7 | 181.9 | 65.9 | 83.1 | 106.2 | 255.2 |

Note: This scenario assumes a continuation beyond 1981 of average annual inflation rates over the past 10 years.

TABLE 26 Estimated Future Parental Expenditures on Children When the First Child Is Born in 1981, High Inflation Scenario (*Expenditures in thousands of dollars*)

| Socioeconomic Status Group | Age Group | One-child Families | Wife's Employment Status: Full-time, Full-year Worker | | | | | | | |
|---|---|---|---|---|---|---|---|---|---|---|
| | | | Two-child Families | | | Three-child Families | | | |
| | | Total | First Child | Second Child | Total | First Child | Second Child | Third Child | Total |
| High | 0–17 | $342.8 | $263.7 | $320.2 | $583.9 | $219.6 | $261.1 | $323.2 | $803.9 |
| | 0–5 | 47.5 | 41.5 | 39.2 | 80.7 | 41.9 | 36.1 | 33.0 | 111.1 |
| | 6–11 | 106.4 | 79.5 | 99.0 | 178.5 | 64.2 | 78.8 | 99.1 | 242.1 |
| | 12–17 | 188.9 | 142.7 | 182.1 | 324.8 | 113.5 | 146.1 | 191.1 | 450.7 |
| Medium | 0–17 | 304.2 | 235.1 | 283.0 | 518.1 | 196.6 | 231.6 | 285.2 | 713.4 |
| | 0–5 | 43.2 | 38.0 | 34.8 | 72.8 | 38.6 | 32.3 | 28.5 | 99.4 |
| | 6–11 | 95.3 | 71.3 | 88.2 | 159.5 | 57.7 | 70.3 | 88.0 | 216.0 |
| | 12–17 | 165.7 | 125.7 | 160.0 | 285.8 | 100.3 | 129.0 | 168.8 | 398.0 |
| Low | 0–17 | 285.9 | 221.4 | 265.8 | 487.2 | 185.5 | 218.0 | 268.1 | 671.6 |
| | 0–5 | 40.8 | 36.1 | 32.5 | 68.5 | 36.8 | 30.3 | 26.2 | 93.3 |
| | 6–11 | 89.9 | 67.3 | 83.0 | 150.4 | 54.5 | 66.3 | 82.9 | 203.6 |
| | 12–17 | 155.2 | 118.1 | 150.3 | 268.3 | 94.3 | 121.4 | 159.1 | 374.7 |

TABLE 26   Estimated Future Parental Expenditures on Children When the First Child Is Born in 1981, High Inflation Scenario (continued)   (Expenditures in thousands of dollars)

| Socioeconomic Status Group | Age Group | One-child Families Total | Wife's Employment Status: Part-time, Full-year Worker | | | | | | | |
|---|---|---|---|---|---|---|---|---|---|---|
| | | | Two-child Families | | | Three-child Families | | | | |
| | | | First Child | Second Child | Total | First Child | Second Child | Third Child | Total |
| High | 0–17 | $322.0 | $247.9 | $303.2 | $551.0 | $206.4 | $247.3 | $308.1 | $761.9 |
| | 0–5 | 42.3 | 37.2 | 35.0 | 72.3 | 37.8 | 32.5 | 29.6 | 100.0 |
| | 6–11 | 99.5 | 74.4 | 93.4 | 167.8 | 60.1 | 74.4 | 94.3 | 228.8 |
| | 12–17 | 180.1 | 136.3 | 174.7 | 311.0 | 108.5 | 140.4 | 184.2 | 433.1 |
| Medium | 0–17 | 266.2 | 206.5 | 248.8 | 455.4 | 173.1 | 204.4 | 252.5 | 630.0 |
| | 0–5 | 36.7 | 32.6 | 29.1 | 61.6 | 33.4 | 27.3 | 23.4 | 84.1 |
| | 6–11 | 83.6 | 62.7 | 77.7 | 140.4 | 50.7 | 62.1 | 78.0 | 190.8 |
| | 12–17 | 145.9 | 111.3 | 142.0 | 253.3 | 89.0 | 115.0 | 151.1 | 355.1 |
| Low | 0–17 | 240.9 | 187.6 | 225.2 | 412.9 | 157.8 | 185.6 | 229.2 | 572.5 |
| | 0–5 | 33.4 | 29.9 | 25.9 | 55.8 | 30.8 | 24.6 | 20.4 | 75.8 |
| | 6–11 | 76.1 | 57.1 | 70.6 | 127.7 | 46.3 | 56.4 | 70.9 | 173.6 |
| | 12–17 | 131.5 | 100.7 | 128.7 | 229.4 | 80.7 | 104.6 | 138.0 | 323.2 |

TABLE 26 (continued) Estimated Future Parental Expenditures on Children When the First Child Is Born in 1981, High Inflation Scenario
(Expenditures in thousands of dollars)

| Socioeconomic Status Group | Age Group | One-child Families Total | Wife's Employment Status: Not Employed | | | | | | | |
|---|---|---|---|---|---|---|---|---|---|---|
| | | | Two-child Families | | | Three-child Families | | | |
| | | | First Child | Second Child | Total | First Child | Second Child | Third Child | Total |
| High | 0-17 | $302.4 | $233.1 | $286.5 | $519.6 | $194.2 | $234.0 | $292.9 | $721.0 |
| | 0-5 | 38.1 | 33.7 | 31.6 | 65.2 | 34.4 | 29.4 | 26.7 | 90.5 |
| | 6-11 | 93.1 | 69.7 | 88.1 | 157.7 | 56.3 | 70.2 | 89.5 | 216.0 |
| | 12-17 | 171.2 | 129.7 | 166.9 | 296.7 | 103.4 | 134.3 | 176.8 | 414.5 |
| Medium | 0-17 | 246.4 | 191.7 | 230.8 | 422.4 | 161.0 | 189.9 | 234.9 | 585.8 |
| | 0-5 | 33.5 | 29.9 | 26.3 | 56.2 | 30.9 | 24.9 | 20.9 | 76.6 |
| | 6-11 | 77.7 | 58.2 | 72.3 | 130.5 | 47.2 | 57.8 | 72.7 | 177.6 |
| | 12-17 | 135.3 | 103.5 | 132.2 | 235.7 | 82.9 | 107.3 | 141.3 | 331.5 |
| Low | 0-17 | 223.5 | 174.5 | 209.4 | 383.9 | 147.0 | 172.9 | 214.0 | 533.9 |
| | 0-5 | 30.6 | 27.5 | 23.5 | 51.0 | 28.6 | 22.4 | 18.2 | 69.1 |
| | 6-11 | 70.8 | 53.1 | 65.8 | 118.9 | 43.1 | 52.6 | 66.2 | 161.9 |
| | 12-17 | 122.2 | 93.9 | 120.2 | 214.1 | 75.4 | 97.9 | 129.6 | 302.9 |

Note: This scenario assumes a continuation beyond 1981 of average annual inflation rates over the past 5 years.

TABLE 27    Total Inflation-adjusted Expenditures from Birth through Four
Years of College for an Average Child in a Medium SES Two-child
Family

| Inflation Assumption | Direct Expenditures to Age 18 [a] | Four Years of College | Total |
|---|---|---|---|
| High | $227,700 | $47,330 [b] | $275,030 |
| | | 82,830 [c] | 310,530 |
| Medium | 199,650 | 47,330 [b] | 246,980 |
| | | 82,830 [c] | 282,480 |
| Low | 149,150 | 47,330 [b] | 196,480 |
| | | 82,830 [c] | 231,980 |

a. Assumes the two children are born in 1981 and 1983 and that the mother works part
time.
b. Projected cost for four years at a state university for a child born in 1976.
c. Projected cost for four years at a private college for a child born in 1976.

tive when applied to children born during the 1980s, the estimates of
$47,330 for four years at a state university and $82,830 for four years at a
private college can be added to our projections of parental expenditures to
age 18 to derive an approximate estimate of total expenditures. The data
for a medium SES family in table 27 indicate that the expenditures associated with rearing a child from birth through four years of college can range
between approximately $196,000 and $310,000, depending on the type
of four-year institution attended and the assumptions regarding future
inflation.

# Appendix
## *Methodology*

This appendix gives the details behind the estimates of child-related parental expenditures reported in chapter 4 and concerns the following topics: a suitable choice for a family standard-of-living index; life-cycle patterns of individual earnings and total family consumption; the distribution of total family spending across various categories of goods and services; and the determinants of changes in family standards of living.

## Choosing an Isoprop Measure

### Background

Of the numerous ways of establishing equivalencies in diverse families' standards of living, one that has gained popularity over the years is reliance on budget shares. Some commodity group is picked, and two families are assumed to have the same standard of living if they spend equal proportions (hence the term isoprop) of their total budget on that commodity group.

For example, Dorothy S. Brady published two scales of equivalent income with the original City Worker's Family Budget (see U.S. Bureau of Labor Statistics, 1948). These scales were designed to show the relative income that families of different sizes would need to maintain equivalent levels of living. For one of the scales, equivalencies were defined in terms of the incomes at which the same percentage of families of each size had an adequate diet. The other scale assumed that two families have the same standard of living if they allocate the same proportion of their income to savings.

Other studies have established equivalencies on the basis of the proportion of income spent on food. Families that spend the same proportion of their income on food are assumed to have equivalent standards of living. Lower proportions correspond to higher standards of living, and vice versa. Numerous claims are made throughout the literature that the proportion of income spent on food is an appropriate index when comparing living standards among families of dissimilar types. Included in these contentions are the following:

> It has long been accepted for individuals as for nations that the proportion of income allocated to the "necessaries," and in particular to food, is an indicator of economic well-being. A declining percentage has been associated with prosperity and higher incomes, and the rising percentage associated with lower income has been taken as an indicator of stringency (Orshansky 1965a: 7).

> With no market basket to demarcate the line below which deprivation is almost inevitable and above which a limited measure of adequacy is at least possible, an adaptation was made of a principle most of us learn by heart: As income increases, families spend more dollars for food, but this larger amount takes a smaller share of income leaving proportionately more money for other things. Accordingly, a low percentage of income going for food can be equated with prosperity and a high percentage with privation. Economists looking for a quick way to assess the relative well-being of dissimilar groups have long resorted to this device (Orshansky 1965b: 8).

The U.S. Social Security Administration has developed two thresholds of poverty "based on the amount needed by families of different size and type to purchase a nutritionally adequate diet on the assumption that no more than a third of family income is used for food" (Orshansky 1969: 38). In addition, the Bureau of Labor Statistics has called the proportion of income spent on food "one of the most generally accepted measures of level of living" (Estimating Equivalent Incomes 1960: 1198), and it has used this measure in devising its scales of equivalent income (see, for example, U.S. Bureau of Labor Statistics 1968). A slight modification of this indicator was used by Espenshade (1973) to infer the level of parental expenditures on children from data contained in the 1960–1961 Survey of Consumer Expenditures (SCE).

In more recent work, Harold W. Watts (1977) has introduced some new perspectives into the use of equivalence scales for the purpose of establishing poverty lines by allowing for geographic variation (specifically, the four Census regions) and urban-rural residence. Watts determines equivalent levels of living in two ways: by the proportion of pretax income spent on food, and on the basic necessities including food, clothing, housing, and transportation. He concludes as follows:

> On the basis of the analysis above, the Iso-Prop Index appears to be a promising approach to the problem of equivalent income levels. It is based on observable behavior; it does not limit itself to price variations alone; and it produces results which are both consistent with a priori notions and, in the case of family size, similar to the equivalence scales estimated by others (p. 199).

In our study we continue the isoprop tradition. The following pages report on various experiments to determine the most satisfactory index.

## Cross-tabular Results

Any isoprop index has a numerator, and it has a denominator. In our preliminary investigations, we focused our evaluation on nine candidates for the numerator and three for the denominator, yielding a total of twenty-seven potential isoprop measures from which to choose. The nine candidates for the numerator included annual household expenditures for total food consumption, food at home, food away from home (including the value of meals received as pay), housing (including shelter, fuel and utilities, telephone, domestic services and materials, and house furnishings and equipment), shelter, clothing (including dry cleaning and laundry), total food plus clothing, food at home plus clothing, and transportation. For a denominator, we experimented with total consumer unit (CU) annual income before taxes, CU annual income after personal taxes, and total CU annual current consumption expenditures.[1]

Our chief concern is to find out how each of these twenty-seven indicators performs as a measure of a family's standard of living. To do this, we constructed cross-tabulations of the data and estimated several regression equations. In this section we report on the cross-tabular results.

All families were first classified by family size (number of children = 0, 1, 2, 3, and 4+) and by annual total current consumption (under $5,000, $5,000-$7,499, $7,500-$9,999, $10,000-$12,499, and $12,500 and over). Then for each cell, the appropriate isoprop measure was constructed by dividing the average value of the numerator by the average value of the denominator, and multiplying by 100. The results for food at home, housing, and transportation expenditures as a percentage of total CU current consumption expenditures are displayed in table A.1.

TABLE A.1 Percentage of Total Current Consumption Expenditure Devoted to Food at Home, Housing, and Transportation in Consumer Units (CUs) with Wife Employed

| Total Current Consumption Expenditure | All Families | Number of Children | | | | |
|---|---|---|---|---|---|---|
| | | 0 | 1 | 2 | 3 | 4+ |
| | | *Food at Home* | | | | |
| Under 5,000 | 19.8 | 14.9 | 19.3 | 24.0 | 27.5 | 30.9 |
| 5,000–7,499 | 17.7 | 12.8 | 16.5 | 20.2 | 23.8 | 26.6 |
| 7,500–9,999 | 16.3 | 11.2 | 14.2 | 18.4 | 20.8 | 24.0 |
| 10,000–12,499 | 15.1 | 8.7 | 13.6 | 16.0 | 18.2 | 21.7 |
| 12,500 and over | 13.0 | 7.4 | 11.0 | 12.7 | 14.0 | 18.0 |
| | | *Housing* | | | | |
| Under 5,000 | 32.6 | 36.7 | 32.9 | 27.7 | 27.4 | 26.3 |
| 5,000–7,499 | 32.0 | 34.0 | 32.3 | 32.4 | 27.9 | 27.6 |
| 7,500–9,999 | 30.4 | 31.8 | 30.9 | 30.5 | 28.4 | 27.6 |
| 10,000–12,499 | 28.5 | 31.1 | 28.8 | 27.9 | 27.4 | 26.6 |
| 12,500 and over | 26.4 | 28.7 | 27.6 | 26.7 | 25.7 | 23.7 |
| | | *Transportation* | | | | |
| Under 5,000 | 16.0 | 15.3 | 17.2 | 16.9 | 14.2 | 13.7 |
| 5,000–7,499 | 17.4 | 18.0 | 18.2 | 16.2 | 16.8 | 16.2 |
| 7,500–9,999 | 19.2 | 21.9 | 20.8 | 17.3 | 16.9 | 15.9 |
| 10,000–12,499 | 22.7 | 25.8 | 24.0 | 22.2 | 20.0 | 20.2 |
| 12,500 and over | 24.5 | 26.5 | 28.2 | 24.2 | 22.7 | 21.8 |

Before commenting on this table or on the other findings, it is first necessary to establish some criteria by which we can evaluate the alternative isoprop measures. For the cross-tabular analysis, we have selected the following criteria:

1. *Monotonicity*. Increases in family size, holding income constant, or increases in income, holding family size constant, should be reflected in monotonic changes in a standard-of-living indicator. That is, the changes in the indicator should be either up or down but not up and down across family sizes or across income levels.

2. *Elasticity*. One would like the measure of living standards to be responsive to changes in income and family size.

3. *Prominence*. The consumption category selected for the numerator should be a comparatively prominent component of total expenditure to keep random fluctuations from dominating the measure.

4. *Consistency*. Increases in family size, holding income constant

should have an impact on the isoprop measure that is opposite in sign from an increase in income, holding family size constant. The rationale for this criterion is that it is reasonable to assume that family living standards will fall if family size increases with no change in income, whereas living standards may be expected to rise if income increases with no change in family size.

5. *Conformity with a priori expectations.* The only two categories of consumption for which previous research leads us to form a priori expectations are total food consumption and food at home. Isoprop measures with either of these items in the numerator may be expected to vary inversely with changes in a family's standard of living. Thus, these measures should increase with increases in family size and decline with increases in income, other things held constant.

The performance of each of the twenty-seven isoprop measures was gauged against these five criteria. In general, measures that contained either total food consumption or food at home in the numerator and either after-tax income or total current consumption in the denominator seemed to be most well-behaved. In table A.1, for example, using food at home for the numerator satisfies all five criteria. Housing exhibits nonmonotonic behavior in families with two or more children. And it also fails on consistency; the housing isoprop index declines both with increases in family size *and* with increases in income. An index based on transportation expenditures performs better than housing but not as well as food at home. Transportation exhibits some nonmonotonic behavior with the effect arising between no children and one child. Clothing expenditures and expenditures for food consumed away from home are not shown in table A.1. Clothing expenditures tended to average between 8 and 9 percent of total family expenditures, and food away from home typically consumed 6 percent or less. Thus, by themselves, they were considered to compose an insufficiently large proportion of the total budget to function well as the numerator of a standard-of-living index.

## Regression Results

Our tentative conclusion, derived from the cross-tabular analysis, is that either food at home or total food works best in the numerator and that total consumption expenditures or after-tax income makes a suitable denominator for an indicator of family standard of living. However, the cross-tabulations ignore several potentially important influences on the behavior of the indicators. Regression analysis can help solve this problem.

In the regressions, alternative isoprop measures were used as dependent variables together with the independent variables shown in table A.2. Tables A.3, A.4, A.5, and A.6 show the results of choosing as the dependent variable the percentage of total current consumption expenditure going to total food (Y11), the percentage of total current consumption going to food at home (Y12), the percentage of after-tax income going to total food (Y21), and the percentage of after-tax income going to food at home (Y22).

The four regressions in tables A.3-A.6 were not the only ones we estimated. All nine of the numerators discussed in the previous section were used again along with STOTEXP and NETINCOM in the denominator. But these four did appear most promising. To arrive at this conclusion and to select a single indicator for our subsequent work, we again needed a set of criteria to guide our choices among the regressions. To develop these criteria we first work from two simple propositions: (1) an increase in the number of family members in any age-sex category, ceteris paribus, lowers a family's standard (or level) of living and (2) an increase in income (or consumption), ceteris paribus, raises the level of living. From these propositions we may deduce that (1) the estimated regression coefficients of the twenty-four age-sex variables should all have the same sign (nothing can be inferred about the relative magnitudes of these coefficients, however, nor whether the signs should be positive or negative) and (2) the coefficient on the total consumption variable (either STOTEXP or NETINCOM) should have the opposite sign.

Therefore, to help further in selecting the most satisfactory indicator of equivalent levels of living, we will concentrate on those regressions that meet the dual criteria of the following:

1. The signs on the age-sex variables are all the same and opposite from the sign on STOTEXP or NETINCOM, and

2. In addition, the estimated coefficients on the age-sex variables and on consumption are statistically significant.

On the basis of these criteria we selected as our isoprop measure the percentage of total current consumption devoted to expenditures on food at home (Y12 in table A.4). We will assume hereafter that if two families allot the same share of their total current consumption expenditures to food at home, then they have the same material standard of living, regardless of differences in family size and composition or in total consumption.

Two final points are worth mentioning. First, we need to emphasize that our choice of a particular isoprop measure was made prior to and therefore independently of the specific estimates of parental expenditures

TABLE A.2  Definitions of Independent Variables Used in Tables A.3, A.4, A.5, A.6

| Variable Type | Variable Name | Definition |
|---|---|---|
| Income | STOTEXP<br>NETINCOM | Total current consumption expenditures.<br>CU annual income after personal taxes. |
| Family size and composition | MALAGE(i)<br>FEMAGE(i)<br><br>i = 1, 2, ..., 12 | The number of full-year equivalent CU members, male and female respectively, in each of 24 age-sex categories. Age groups used are under 1, 1-2, 3-5, 6-8, 9-11, 12-14, 15-17, 18-24, 25-34, 35-44, 45-54, and 55 and over.[a] |
| Geographic region | NORTHCEN<br>SOUTH<br>WEST | Dummy variables for North Central, South, and West census regions. East is the excluded category. |
| Race | BLACK | BLACK = 1 if race of CU head is black; 0 otherwise. |
| Residence | NONMETRO | NONMETRO = 1 if CU is located outside an SMSA; 0 otherwise. |
| Survey year | SY73 | SY73 = 1 if 1973; 0 if 1972. |
| Employment status | WORKFULL<br>WORKPART<br>WORKNR | Wife usually worked full time, when working.<br>Wife usually worked part time, when working.<br>Wife's employment status not reported. (Each of the employment status variables is coded as a dummy variable; wives who did not work during the survey year constitute the excluded category.) |
| Education | EDUCELEM<br><br>EDUCCOLL<br>EDUCNR | CU head has less than a high school education.<br>CU head had at least some college completed.<br>Education of CU head not reported. (Each of the education variables is coded as a dummy variable; CU heads who were high school graduates are the excluded category.) |
| Occupation | OCCUBLUE<br>OCCUMISC | CU head is a wage or other salaried worker.<br>CU head is not working, retired, or other. (Each occupation variable is coded as a dummy variable; CU heads who were self employed; salaried professional, technical and kindred workers; or salaried managers and administrators constitute the excluded category.) |

a. The reason for introducing the "full-year equivalent" qualifier before CU members is that some persons are not CU members the entire year. If an individual is in the household for only 6 months (in the case of a newborn child, for example), that person counts as 0.5 family members insofar as his or her impact on annual consumption patterns is concerned.

*Appendix*

TABLE A.3   Regressions for Selecting a Standard-of-living Indicator: Dependent Variable (Y11) = Percentage of Total Current Consumption Expenditures Devoted to Total Food

| MODEL: MODEL01 | | SSE | 688987.3 | F RATIO | 89.50 |
|---|---|---|---|---|---|
| | | DFE | 8908 | PROB>F | 0.0001 |
| DEP VAR: Y11 | | MSE | 77.344784 | R-SQUARE | 0.2815 |

| Variable | DF | Parameter Estimate | Standard Error | T Ratio | PROB > \|T\| |
|---|---|---|---|---|---|
| INTERCEPT | 1 | 19.051749 | 0.576322 | 33.0575 | 0.0001 |
| STOTEXP | 1 | −0.000545643 | 0.0000196959 | −27.7034 | 0.0001 |
| MALAGE1 | 1 | −1.999152 | 0.638511 | −3.1310 | 0.0017 |
| MALAGE2 | 1 | 0.737943 | 0.359634 | 2.0519 | 0.0402 |
| MALAGE3 | 1 | 1.798982 | 0.277535 | 6.4820 | 0.0001 |
| MALAGE4 | 1 | 2.211990 | 0.259643 | 8.5193 | 0.0001 |
| MALAGE5 | 1 | 2.227208 | 0.253333 | 8.7916 | 0.0001 |
| MALAGE6 | 1 | 2.666591 | 0.244757 | 10.8949 | 0.0001 |
| MALAGE7 | 1 | 2.415759 | 0.262427 | 9.2054 | 0.0001 |
| MALAGE8 | 1 | 0.583662 | 0.238379 | 2.4485 | 0.0144 |
| MALAGE9 | 1 | 2.198380 | 0.383402 | 5.7339 | 0.0001 |
| MALAGE10 | 1 | 3.985695 | 0.465607 | 8.5602 | 0.0001 |
| MALAGE11 | 1 | 4.980415 | 0.513585 | 9.6974 | 0.0001 |
| MALAGE12 | 1 | 5.926196 | 0.610902 | 9.7007 | 0.0001 |
| FEMAGE1 | 1 | −0.378802 | 0.658588 | −0.5752 | 0.5652 |
| FEMAGE2 | 1 | 0.593322 | 0.345883 | 1.7154 | 0.0863 |
| FEMAGE3 | 1 | 1.284784 | 0.289199 | 4.4426 | 0.0001 |
| FEMAGE4 | 1 | 1.848977 | 0.267435 | 6.9137 | 0.0001 |
| FEMAGE5 | 1 | 1.601649 | 0.252523 | 6.3426 | 0.0001 |
| FEMAGE6 | 1 | 2.283825 | 0.253882 | 8.9956 | 0.0001 |
| FEMAGE7 | 1 | 1.508028 | 0.267387 | 5.6399 | 0.0001 |
| FEMAGE8 | 1 | 0.135033 | 0.264146 | 0.5112 | 0.6092 |
| FEMAGE9 | 1 | 2.605869 | 0.400979 | 6.4988 | 0.0001 |
| FEMAGE10 | 1 | 3.794299 | 0.476098 | 7.9696 | 0.0001 |
| FEMAGE11 | 1 | 4.057341 | 0.534056 | 7.5972 | 0.0001 |
| FEMAGE12 | 1 | 4.051086 | 0.672169 | 6.0269 | 0.0001 |
| NORTHCEN | 1 | −1.665694 | 0.268518 | −6.2033 | 0.0001 |
| SOUTH | 1 | −0.595029 | 0.271534 | −2.1914 | 0.0285 |
| WEST | 1 | −1.274087 | 0.289944 | −4.3943 | 0.0001 |
| BLACK | 1 | −0.785885 | 0.380334 | −2.0663 | 0.0388 |
| NONMETRO | 1 | −0.143888 | 0.211655 | −0.6798 | 0.4966 |
| SY73 | 1 | 0.879221 | 0.187212 | 4.6964 | 0.0001 |
| WORKFULL | 1 | −1.329787 | 0.221636 | −5.9999 | 0.0001 |
| WORKPART | 1 | −0.871097 | 0.271321 | −3.2106 | 0.0013 |
| WORKNR | 1 | 0.502709 | 0.637172 | 0.7890 | 0.4302 |
| EDUCELEM | 1 | 0.947714 | 0.244573 | 3.8750 | 0.0001 |
| EDUCCOLL | 1 | −1.436903 | 0.242395 | −5.9279 | 0.0001 |
| EDUCNR | 1 | −0.189383 | 0.731851 | −0.2588 | 0.7958 |
| OCCUBLUE | 1 | 0.667968 | 0.226711 | 2.9463 | 0.0032 |
| OCCUMISC | 1 | 0.832335 | 0.393456 | 2.1154 | 0.0344 |

*Methodology* 95

TABLE A.4 Regressions for Selecting a Standard-of-living Indicator: Dependent Variable (Y12) = Percentage of Total Current Consumption Expenditures Devoted to Food at Home

| MODEL: MODEL01 | | SSE | 595214.7 | F RATIO | 117.59 |
|---|---|---|---|---|---|
| | | DFE | 8908 | PROB>F | 0.0001 |
| DEP VAR: Y12 | | MSE | 66.817999 | R-SQUARE | 0.3399 |

| Variable | DF | Parameter Estimate | Standard Error | T Ratio | PROB>\|T\| |
|---|---|---|---|---|---|
| INTERCEPT | 1 | 14.050004 | 0.535669 | 26.2289 | 0.0001 |
| STOTEXP | 1 | −0.000570401 | .00001830657 | −31.1583 | 0.0001 |
| MALAGE1 | 1 | −0.870389 | 0.593471 | −1.4666 | 0.1425 |
| MALAGE2 | 1 | 1.323292 | 0.334266 | 3.9588 | 0.0001 |
| MALAGE3 | 1 | 2.432820 | 0.257958 | 9.4311 | 0.0001 |
| MALAGE4 | 1 | 2.487683 | 0.241329 | 10.3083 | 0.0001 |
| MALAGE5 | 1 | 2.303476 | 0.235463 | 9.7827 | 0.0001 |
| MALAGE6 | 1 | 2.619217 | 0.227492 | 11.5135 | 0.0001 |
| MALAGE7 | 1 | 2.264671 | 0.243916 | 9.2846 | 0.0001 |
| MALAGE8 | 1 | 0.622933 | 0.221564 | 2.8115 | 0.0049 |
| MALAGE9 | 1 | 1.765126 | 0.356358 | 4.9532 | 0.0001 |
| MALAGE10 | 1 | 3.515509 | 0.432764 | 8.1234 | 0.0001 |
| MALAGE11 | 1 | 4.555965 | 0.477357 | 9.5441 | 0.0001 |
| MALAGE12 | 1 | 5.517263 | 0.567309 | 9.7168 | 0.0001 |
| FEMAGE1 | 1 | 0.642501 | 0.612132 | 1.0496 | 0.2939 |
| FEMAGE2 | 1 | 1.447915 | 0.321485 | 4.5038 | 0.0001 |
| FEMAGE3 | 1 | 1.691954 | 0.268799 | 6.2945 | 0.0001 |
| FEMAGE4 | 1 | 2.103562 | 0.248570 | 8.4626 | 0.0001 |
| FEMAGE5 | 1 | 1.743857 | 0.234710 | 7.4298 | 0.0001 |
| FEMAGE6 | 1 | 2.436738 | 0.235974 | 10.3263 | 0.0001 |
| FEMAGE7 | 1 | 1.498154 | 0.248526 | 6.0282 | 0.0001 |
| FEMAGE8 | 1 | 0.485538 | 0.245513 | 1.9776 | 0.0480 |
| FEMAGE9 | 1 | 2.957250 | 0.372694 | 7.9348 | 0.0001 |
| FEMAGE10 | 1 | 4.242759 | 0.442515 | 9.5878 | 0.0001 |
| FEMAGE11 | 1 | 4.978977 | 0.496385 | 10.0305 | 0.0001 |
| FEMAGE12 | 1 | 4.937595 | 0.624755 | 7.9032 | 0.0001 |
| NORTHCEN | 1 | −1.757941 | 0.249577 | −7.0437 | 0.0001 |
| SOUTH | 1 | −1.145223 | 0.252380 | −4.5377 | 0.0001 |
| WEST | 1 | −1.340639 | 0.269492 | −4.9747 | 0.0001 |
| BLACK | 1 | 0.045695 | 0.353506 | 0.1293 | 0.8972 |
| NONMETRO | 1 | 0.462096 | 0.196725 | 2.3489 | 0.0188 |
| SY73 | 1 | 0.753323 | 0.174006 | 4.3293 | 0.0001 |
| WORKFULL | 1 | −2.157618 | 0.206002 | −10.4738 | 0.0001 |
| WORKPART | 1 | −0.979469 | 0.252183 | −3.8840 | 0.0001 |
| WORKNR | 1 | −0.718529 | 0.592227 | −1.2133 | 0.2251 |
| EDUCELEM | 1 | 1.109648 | 0.227321 | 4.8814 | 0.0001 |
| EDUCCOLL | 1 | −1.365267 | 0.225297 | −6.0599 | 0.0001 |
| EDUCNR | 1 | 0.132306 | 0.680227 | 0.1945 | 0.8458 |
| OCCUBLUE | 1 | 1.070083 | 0.210719 | 5.0783 | 0.0001 |
| OCCUMISC | 1 | 2.341276 | 0.365702 | 6.4021 | 0.0001 |

TABLE A.5   Regressions for Selecting a Standard-of-living Indicator: Dependent Variable (Y21) = Percentage of After-tax Income Devoted to Total Food

| MODEL: MODEL02 | | SSE | 77653451 | F RATIO | 4.96 |
|---|---|---|---|---|---|
| | | DFE | 8908 | PROB>F | 0.0001 |
| DEP VAR: Y21 | | MSE | 8717.271 | R-SQUARE | 0.0212 |

| Variable | DF | Parameter Estimate | Standard Error | T Ratio | PROB > \|T\| |
|---|---|---|---|---|---|
| INTERCEPT | 1 | 24.570192 | 6.046928 | 4.0633 | 0.0001 |
| NETINCOM | 1 | −0.000398744 | 0.0001195275 | −7.5191 | 0.0001 |
| MALAGE1 | 1 | −7.677626 | 6.777392 | −1.1328 | 0.2573 |
| MALAGE2 | 1 | −3.657065 | 3.817918 | −0.9579 | 0.3382 |
| MALAGE3 | 1 | −1.277056 | 2.945675 | −0.4335 | 0.6646 |
| MALAGE4 | 1 | 3.720173 | 2.756453 | 1.3496 | 0.1772 |
| MALAGE5 | 1 | 4.153528 | 2.688375 | 1.5450 | 0.1224 |
| MALAGE6 | 1 | −1.571245 | 2.597751 | −0.6048 | 0.5453 |
| MALAGE7 | 1 | 10.994148 | 2.780802 | 3.9536 | 0.0001 |
| MALAGE8 | 1 | 8.404412 | 2.526239 | 3.3268 | 0.0009 |
| MALAGE9 | 1 | 7.770908 | 4.079110 | 1.9050 | 0.0568 |
| MALAGE10 | 1 | 1.008013 | 4.963811 | 0.2031 | 0.8391 |
| MALAGE11 | 1 | 7.763138 | 5.477405 | 1.4173 | 0.1564 |
| MALAGE12 | 1 | 3.966484 | 6.506674 | 0.6096 | 0.5421 |
| FEMAGE1 | 1 | −3.099757 | 6.989470 | −0.4435 | 0.6574 |
| FEMAGE2 | 1 | −4.632226 | 3.671968 | −1.2615 | 0.2072 |
| FEMAGE3 | 1 | −0.558523 | 3.070286 | −0.1819 | 0.8557 |
| FEMAGE4 | 1 | −1.713295 | 2.839385 | −0.6034 | 0.5463 |
| FEMAGE5 | 1 | 2.857745 | 2.680003 | 1.0663 | 0.2863 |
| FEMAGE6 | 1 | −1.013265 | 2.694052 | −0.3761 | 0.7068 |
| FEMAGE7 | 1 | 6.873250 | 2.833139 | 2.4260 | 0.0153 |
| FEMAGE8 | 1 | −1.220400 | 2.785019 | −0.4382 | 0.6613 |
| FEMAGE9 | 1 | 5.295773 | 4.238596 | 1.2494 | 0.2115 |
| FEMAGE10 | 1 | 4.930002 | 5.040605 | 0.9781 | 0.3281 |
| FEMAGE11 | 1 | −1.563577 | 5.663758 | −0.2761 | 0.7825 |
| FEMAGE12 | 1 | −2.587931 | 7.134953 | −0.3627 | 0.7168 |
| NORTHCEN | 1 | −3.530426 | 2.851723 | −1.2380 | 0.2157 |
| SOUTH | 1 | 0.239718 | 2.880952 | 0.0832 | 0.9337 |
| WEST | 1 | −4.623431 | 3.080678 | −1.5008 | 0.1334 |
| BLACK | 1 | 1.167225 | 4.035222 | 0.2893 | 0.7724 |
| NONMETRO | 1 | −0.466994 | 2.239894 | −0.2085 | 0.8349 |
| SY73 | 1 | 3.481063 | 1.987873 | 1.7511 | 0.0800 |
| WORKFULL | 1 | −8.702129 | 2.356939 | −3.6921 | 0.0002 |
| WORKPART | 1 | −6.723506 | 2.880333 | −2.3343 | 0.0196 |
| WORKNR | 1 | −4.580532 | 6.765073 | −0.6771 | 0.4984 |
| EDUCELEM | 1 | 1.754543 | 2.596757 | 0.6757 | 0.4993 |
| EDUCCOLL | 1 | 0.623252 | 2.570452 | 0.2425 | 0.8084 |
| EDUCNR | 1 | −2.822723 | 7.765455 | −0.3635 | 0.7162 |
| OCCUBLUE | 1 | −0.883082 | 2.408656 | −0.3666 | 0.7139 |
| OCCUMISC | 1 | 24.103008 | 4.198342 | 5.7411 | 0.0001 |

TABLE A.6  Regressions for Selecting a Standard-of-living Indicator: Dependent Variable (Y22) = Percentage of After-tax Income Devoted to Food at Home

| MODEL: MODEL02 | | SSE | 46627605 | F RATIO | 5.85 |
|---|---|---|---|---|---|
| | | DFE | 8908 | PROB>F | 0.0001 |
| DEP VAR: Y22 | | MSE | 5234.352 | R-SQUARE | 0.0250 |

| Variable | DF | Parameter Estimate | Standard Error | T Ratio | PROB > \|T\| |
|---|---|---|---|---|---|
| INTERCEPT | 1 | 17.556637 | 4.685716 | 3.7468 | 0.0002 |
| NETINCOM | 1 | −0.000744157 | .00009262088 | −8.0344 | 0.0001 |
| MALAGE1 | 1 | −4.670625 | 5.251747 | −0.8893 | 0.3738 |
| MALAGE2 | 1 | −2.111994 | 2.958474 | −0.7139 | 0.4753 |
| MALAGE3 | 1 | 0.222636 | 2.282580 | 0.0975 | 0.9223 |
| MALAGE4 | 1 | 3.634107 | 2.135953 | 1.7014 | 0.0889 |
| MALAGE5 | 1 | 3.483644 | 2.083200 | 1.6723 | 0.0945 |
| MALAGE6 | 1 | −0.865667 | 2.012976 | −0.4300 | 0.6672 |
| MALAGE7 | 1 | 8.617223 | 2.154821 | 3.9990 | 0.0001 |
| MALAGE8 | 1 | 6.407528 | 1.957563 | 3.2732 | 0.0011 |
| MALAGE9 | 1 | 6.390861 | 3.160870 | 2.0219 | 0.0432 |
| MALAGE10 | 1 | 1.438321 | 3.846417 | 0.3739 | 0.7085 |
| MALAGE11 | 1 | 7.340113 | 4.244397 | 1.7294 | 0.0838 |
| MALAGE12 | 1 | 4.728791 | 5.041970 | 0.9379 | 0.3483 |
| FEMAGE1 | 1 | −0.948448 | 5.416084 | −0.1751 | 0.8610 |
| FEMAGE2 | 1 | −2.335680 | 2.845379 | −0.8209 | 0.4117 |
| FEMAGE3 | 1 | 0.542831 | 2.379140 | 0.2282 | 0.8195 |
| FEMAGE4 | 1 | −0.746270 | 2.200217 | −0.3392 | 0.7345 |
| FEMAGE5 | 1 | 2.827111 | 2.076713 | 1.3613 | 0.1734 |
| FEMAGE6 | 1 | −0.228957 | 2.037599 | −0.1097 | 0.9127 |
| FEMAGE7 | 1 | 5.608996 | 2.195376 | 2.5549 | 0.0106 |
| FEMAGE8 | 1 | −1.224585 | 2.158089 | −0.5674 | 0.5704 |
| FEMAGE9 | 1 | 4.659415 | 3.284454 | 1.4186 | 0.1560 |
| FEMAGE10 | 1 | 5.138418 | 3.905924 | 1.3155 | 0.1884 |
| FEMAGE11 | 1 | 0.404223 | 4.388801 | 0.0921 | 0.9266 |
| FEMAGE12 | 1 | −0.105973 | 5.528818 | −0.0192 | 0.9847 |
| NORTHCEN | 1 | −3.394502 | 2.209777 | −1.5361 | 0.1245 |
| SOUTH | 1 | −0.646773 | 2.232426 | −0.2897 | 0.7720 |
| WEST | 1 | −3.867685 | 2.387192 | −1.6202 | 0.1052 |
| BLACK | 1 | 1.851320 | 3.126862 | 0.5921 | 0.5538 |
| NONMETRO | 1 | 0.392493 | 1.735676 | 0.2261 | 0.8211 |
| SY73 | 1 | 2.692940 | 1.540387 | 1.7482 | 0.0805 |
| WORKFULL | 1 | −7.356307 | 1.826373 | −4.0278 | 0.0001 |
| WORKPART | 1 | −5.200879 | 2.231947 | −2.3302 | 0.0198 |
| WORKNR | 1 | −4.201665 | 5.242201 | −0.8015 | 0.4229 |
| EDUCELEM | 1 | 1.596913 | 2.012207 | 0.7936 | 0.4274 |
| EDUCCOLL | 1 | −0.233367 | 1.991823 | −0.1172 | 0.9067 |
| EDUCNR | 1 | −1.654569 | 6.017389 | −0.2750 | 0.7833 |
| OCCUBLUE | 1 | −0.263615 | 1.866448 | −0.1412 | 0.8877 |
| OCCUMISC | 1 | 19.866912 | 3.253261 | 6.1068 | 0.0001 |

on children this indicator subsequently yielded. Second, there is ample jus-
tification in tables A.3-A.6 for preferring STOTEXP over NETINCOM as
the denominator of our standard-of-living indicator. But in addition, we
might prefer STOTEXP because it is a better measure of permanent income than NETINCOM. On this point Marilyn Moon and Eugene Smolensky (1977) have contended as follows:

> In addition, year-to-year fluctuations in total income cast serious doubt on the
> use of money income in any one year as the appropriate measure of economic
> welfare. Permanent income or life-cycle measures smooth out these fluctua-
> tions, yielding a more reasonable estimate of what a family could consume in
> any one year (p. 47).

## Projecting Family Consumption Over the Life Cycle

In this section we address the problem of projecting total family consumption in each year over the life cycle, which is key to estimating the
level of parental expenditures on children. Our strategy is first to estimate
total family consumption and then to distribute this total to parents and
children. At the same time, we are handicapped in efforts because we have
access only to cross-sectional data collected at one point in time. Thus we
cannot actually follow the same families or households over time. Instead,
we rely on *synthetic* life-cycle consumption streams. In other words, we
assume that the 1972-1973 behavior of families with older heads of households is an accurate reflection of how families with younger heads in 1972-
1973 will behave when they reach correspondingly older ages. This assumption also means that our initial estimates of family life-cycle consumption
and of children's consumption will be in terms of prices and incomes prevailing in 1972-1973.

In projecting a family's total current consumption expenditure in any
given year of that family's life cycle, our underlying hypothesis is that consumption depends on two factors: (1) resources available for consumption
and (2) claims against those resources. The chief source of resources available for consumption is the earnings of the husband and (possibly) of the
wife, whereas the number of family members together with their ages reflects the primary claims on those earnings. In what follows we first describe our procedures for estimating separate earnings functions for husbands and wives and then proceed to estimate total family consumption as
a function of available resources and claims against them.

# Husband's Earnings

In 1972–1973 most male heads of husband-wife households worked full time (thirty-five hours or more per week) for most weeks out of the year. Of all 8,547 husbands, 91.3 percent reported that they usually worked full time when working, and just 3.4 percent said they did not work at all. Fewer than 20 percent reported working less than forty-eight weeks during the survey year, and just 7.0 percent said they had less than twenty-six weeks of paid employment. Husbands averaged $11,795 in annual earnings in 1972–1973.

In light of this behavior, we assume that variations in husband's earnings are mainly because of differences in hourly wage rates. The 1972–1973 Consumer Expenditure Survey (CES) contains information on annual earnings but not on annual hours worked. Therefore we cannot compute hourly wage rates, either for husbands or for wives. For husbands, we assume that hourly wage rates are determined by experience and by a combination of education and occupation variables. Specifically, we let husband's earnings (YH) depend on husband's age and age squared and estimate this relationship within each of several education-occupation groups. The groups are the same as those defined in table A.2. Instead of splitting the sample by education and occupation categories, however, we have estimated just one equation where husbands in white-collar jobs and with a high school education are taken as the reference group, and we have then let other education-occupation combinations influence the intercept and slopes of this regression.

Our husband's earnings function, estimated on the total sample, is shown in table A.7. In general, earnings increase with age up to some maximum and then decline.

# Wife's Earnings

In contrast to their husbands, wives in 1972–1973 exhibited significantly less attachment to the paid labor market. The distribution of wives by their employment status in 1972 or 1973 and by the number of weeks worked is shown in table A.8. Between 40 and 45 percent of wives reported no market work at all during the survey year.

To estimate an earnings function for wives, we restricted our attention to women who reported their education in 1973 (the only year wives' education was asked) and who had some market work. There were 2,337 such women. Wife's earnings (YW) were assumed to be a function of wife's age

TABLE A.7    Equation for Husband's Earnings: Total United States (N = 8547)

| MODEL: EQ42 | | SSE | 4241498722 | F RATIO | 125.78 |
|---|---|---|---|---|---|
| WEIGHT: WEIGHT | | DFE | 8529 | PROB>F | 0.0001 |
| DEP VAR: YH | | MSE | 497303.2 | R-SQUARE | 0.2005 |

| Variable | DF | Parameter Estimate | Standard Error | T Ratio | PROB>\|T\| |
|---|---|---|---|---|---|
| INTERCEPT | 1 | −13.387712 | 2.807568 | −4.7684 | 0.0001 |
| AGE1 | 1 | 1.225138 | 0.145409 | 8.4255 | 0.0001 |
| AGESQR | 1 | −0.012550 | 0.001791053 | −7.0071 | 0.0001 |
| EDUCELEM | 1 | 3.848237 | 2.722978 | 1.4132 | 0.1576 |
| EDUCCOLL | 1 | −12.607447 | 2.792159 | −4.5153 | 0.0001 |
| EDUCNR | 1 | 0.281528 | 6.698717 | 0.0420 | 0.9665 |
| OCCUBLUE | 1 | 7.357746 | 2.761671 | 2.6642 | 0.0077 |
| OCCUMISC | 1 | 16.200398 | 3.741610 | 4.3298 | 0.0001 |
| EDELAG12 | 1 | 0.003371315 | 0.001689856 | 1.9950 | 0.0461 |
| EDCOAG12 | 1 | −0.00700068 | 0.001842337 | −3.7999 | 0.0001 |
| EDNRAG12 | 1 | 0.0006265019 | 0.00400207 | 0.1565 | 0.8756 |
| BLUAGE12 | 1 | 0.00310183 | 0.001774483 | 1.7480 | 0.0805 |
| MSCAGE12 | 1 | 0.009285813 | 0.002120064 | 4.3800 | 0.0001 |
| BLUEAGE1 | 1 | −0.396437 | 0.143589 | −2.7609 | 0.0058 |
| MISCAGE1 | 1 | −1.024330 | 0.183675 | −5.5769 | 0.0001 |
| EDELAG1 | 1 | −0.298113 | 0.138615 | −2.1507 | 0.0315 |
| EDCOAG1 | 1 | 0.678979 | 0.147434 | 4.6053 | 0.0001 |
| EDNRAG1 | 1 | −0.100019 | 0.335858 | −0.2978 | 0.7659 |

Note: AGE1 = Husband's age; AGESQR = Husband's age squared. Variable names terminating with AG1 or AGE1 indicate interactions with AGE1. Those ending with AG12 or AGE12 represent interactions with AGESQR.

(AW), wife's education (same categories as husband's education), and wife's employment. Wife's employment was coded into several dummy variables. D1 equals 1 if the wife works full time for part of the year (less than forty-eight weeks); D2 equals 1 if the wife works on a part-time basis for a full year (forty-eight weeks or more); and D3 equals 1 if the wife works part time for part of the year. In this configuration, the reference group is wives who work full time for forty-eight weeks or more.

The estimated wife's earnings function is shown in table A.9. It was chosen after experimentation with other specifications involving interactions between employment and age, and education and employment interacted with wife's age squared. In table A.9, wife's earnings are positively related to wife's age, with a greater return to education the older the woman. Part-time or part-year employment results in a substantial reduction in annual earnings.

*Methodology*

TABLE A.8 Distribution of Wives in the 1972–1973 Consumer Expenditure Survey (CES) by Employment Status and by Weeks Worked in the Survey Year

*Employment Status*

| Category | Frequency | Cumulative Frequency | Percentage | Cumulative Percentage |
|---|---|---|---|---|
| Did not work | 3735 | 3735 | 43.7 | 43.7 |
| Worked full time[a] | 3175 | 6910 | 37.1 | 80.8 |
| Worked part time[b] | 1441 | 8351 | 16.9 | 97.7 |
| Not reported | 196 | 8547 | 2.3 | 100.0 |

*Weeks Worked*

| Category | Frequency | Cumulative Frequency | Percentage | Cumulative Percentage |
|---|---|---|---|---|
| 0 weeks | 3713 | 3713 | 43.4 | 43.4 |
| 1–9 | 454 | 4167 | 5.3 | 48.8 |
| 10–19 | 502 | 4669 | 5.9 | 54.6 |
| 20–29 | 494 | 5163 | 5.8 | 60.4 |
| 30–39 | 514 | 5677 | 6.0 | 66.4 |
| 40–49 | 600 | 6277 | 7.0 | 73.4 |
| 50–52 | 2172 | 8449 | 25.4 | 98.9 |
| Not reported | 98 | 8547 | 1.1 | 100.0 |

a. Usually worked full time (35 hours or more per week) when working.
b. Usually worked part time (less than 35 hours per week) when working.

TABLE A.9 Equation for Wife's Earnings: Total United States (N = 2337)

| MODEL: EQ14 | | SSE | 102204610 | F RATIO | 366.93 |
|---|---|---|---|---|---|
| WEIGHT: WEIGHT | | DFE | 2330 | PROB>F | 0.0001 |
| DEP VAR: YW | | MSE | 43864.64 | R-SQUARE | 0.4858 |

| Variable | DF | Parameter Estimate | Standard Error | T Ratio | PROB>\|T\| |
|---|---|---|---|---|---|
| INTERCEPT | 1 | 5.615106 | 0.207463 | 27.0656 | 0.0001 |
| AW | 1 | 0.020284 | 0.005563089 | 3.6462 | 0.0003 |
| AWELEM | 1 | −0.015390 | 0.003481088 | −4.4211 | 0.0001 |
| AWCOLL | 1 | 0.050743 | 0.00344566 | 14.7266 | 0.0001 |
| D1 | 1 | −3.345033 | 0.128937 | −25.9431 | 0.0001 |
| D2 | 1 | −4.159712 | 0.182158 | −22.8357 | 0.0001 |
| D3 | 1 | −5.499571 | 0.139154 | −39.5214 | 0.0001 |

## Family Total Consumption Spending

As mentioned earlier, we hypothesize that total family consumption spending (C) depends both on resources available for consumption and on family size and composition. Family composition is captured by twelve age variables, AGES(1), ..., AGES(12), where AGES(i) is the number of full-year equivalent CU members in each of the twelve age groups defined in table A.2.[2] Resources available for consumption are reflected by husband's and wife's earnings.

Our estimated family consumption function is shown in table A.10. Husband's earnings (YH) and wife's earnings (YW) are included separately to allow for the possibility that households may possess different marginal propensities to consume out of YH and YW. Since it is also reasonable to suppose that the marginal propensity to consume from husband's (wife's) earnings depends on the level of wife's (husband's) earnings, if for no other reason than the progressive nature of marginal tax rates, we have included the product of spouses' earnings (YHYW) as a separate variable. The results indicate that there is a positive marginal propensity to consume from both husband's and wife's earnings, and that this marginal propensity is less the higher the spouse's income.

In other regressions not shown here, it was apparent that the addition

TABLE A.10   Equation for Total Family Consumption: Total United States (N = 8547)

| MODEL: MODEL14 | | SSE | 1118788315 | F RATIO | 383.48 |
|---|---|---|---|---|---|
| WEIGHT: WEIGHT | | DFE | 8535 | PROB>F | 0.0001 |
| DEP VAR: C | | MSE | 131082.4 | R-SQUARE | 0.3308 |

| Variable | DF | Parameter Estimate | Standard Error | T Ratio | PROB>\|T\| |
|---|---|---|---|---|---|
| INTERCEPT | 1 | 0.898718 | 0.229583 | 3.9146 | 0.0001 |
| YH | 1 | 0.308337 | 0.006501502 | 47.4254 | 0.0001 |
| YW | 1 | 0.574954 | 0.021993 | 26.1420 | 0.0001 |
| YHYW | 1 | −0.022988 | 0.001359214 | −16.9125 | 0.0001 |
| AGES5 | 1 | 0.280854 | 0.087548 | 3.2080 | 0.0013 |
| AGES6 | 1 | 0.304313 | 0.089773 | 3.3898 | 0.0007 |
| AGES7 | 1 | 0.695005 | 0.095621 | 7.2683 | 0.0001 |
| AGES8 | 1 | 1.844252 | 0.091346 | 20.1896 | 0.0001 |
| AGES9 | 1 | 2.157279 | 0.126302 | 17.0803 | 0.0001 |
| AGES10 | 1 | 2.111264 | 0.125922 | 16.7665 | 0.0001 |
| AGES11 | 1 | 1.931646 | 0.112537 | 17.1645 | 0.0001 |
| AGES12 | 1 | 1.778009 | 0.142783 | 12.4525 | 0.0001 |

of a child under the age of 9 to a family made no appreciable difference to the family's total consumption spending, holding other things constant. Therefore, the equation in table A.10 was estimated by including age variables only for family members age 9 and older. The signs of the estimated coefficients confirm our hypothesis that family consumption spending will increase, holding income constant, the greater the number of family members. Adults in the age range 25-44 appear to have the largest consumption requirements, as measured by the relative sizes of the estimated coefficients on the age variables.

## Simulating Family Consumption

One of the major goals of this research project is to provide data for parenthood education. Young couples who are contemplating having children need better information about the financial responsibilities they are likely to incur through choices about the number, timing, and spacing of their children. Moreover, those who are already parents need some way of anticipating future expenditures on their children.

If this research is to achieve that objective, then we must define prototypical family types with which couples can identify. The potential number of such family types we could conceivably consider has already surpassed manageable limits. Husbands can belong to one of three education groups (less than high school, high school, or more than high school completed) and to one of two occupation categories (blue collar or white collar). Six education-occupation combinations are therefore possible just by considering the husband's characteristics. Wives can also belong to the same three education categories. In addition, five employment status groups are possible including wife does not work, works part time part year, works part time full year, works full time part year, and works full time full year. These education-employment combinations yield thirteen alternative earnings streams for wives (if a wife does not work her earnings are zero regardless of her education attainment). Thus, considering only the socioeconomic characteristics of husbands and wives, 78 ( $= 6 \times 13$) different family types could be defined. Of course, permitting variations in such family demographic characteristics as the number of children, the spacing between them, the age at which a mother has her first child, and the difference in age between husbands and wives complicates the picture even more.

Some way is needed to reduce the number of prototypical family types considered and to select those that are most likely to arise in practice. In table A.11 we display the distribution of the 8,547 husbands in our sample by their reported educational attainment and occupation during the survey year. It is apparent that three cells stand out in terms of their frequency of occurrence: (1) elementary education and blue-collar occupation (20.8 percent of the total ); (2) high school education and blue-collar occupation (24.5 percent); and (3) college education and white-collar occupation (22.8 percent). Taken together, these three family types comprise over two-thirds (68.2 percent) of all husband-wife families in our sample. To focus the analysis, we will present results only for those prototypical families whose husbands fall into one of these three education-occupation categories. Moreover, we will adopt the convention of referring to each of these socioeconomic status categories as low, medium, and high, respectively.

Regarding wives, we will assume they have the same educational attainment as their husbands. Further, in discussing results, we will limit our presentation to wives who either do no market work at all outside the home or who work all year (whether full time or part time). Thus, each of the three socioeconomic status categories can be paired with one of three employment status categories for the wife, giving us a total of nine family types differentiated by socioeconomic characteristics.

To show the implications of our estimated equations for husband's earnings (HY), wife's earnings (YW), and total family spending (C), we have simulated these values together with family income (assumed to be

TABLE A.11    Distribution of Husbands by Education and Occupation, 1972–1973

| Education Group[a] | Occupation[b] | | | |
|---|---|---|---|---|
| | *White Collar* | *Blue Collar* | *Miscellaneous* | *Total* |
| Elementary | 351 | 1779 | 203 | 2333 |
| High School | 799 | 2098 | 181 | 3078 |
| College | 1948 | 882 | 166 | 2996 |
| Not reported | 49 | 78 | 13 | 140 |
| Total | 3147 | 4837 | 563 | 8547 |

a. Education of CU Head refers to highest level of regular schooling completed. Elementary signifies some grade school completed or some high school completed. High school signifies high school graduate. College implies some college completed or college graduate or graduate work.

b. White collar includes self employed, including farm operators; salaried professional, technical and kindred workers; and salaried managers and administrators, and kindred workers. Blue collar includes such wage and other salaried workers as clerical workers, sales workers, craftsmen, operatives, unskilled laborers including household workers, and service workers. Miscellaneous includes not working (not retired), retired, and other (armed forces living off post, working without pay, invalid codes, not reported).

the sum of YH and YW) and the fraction of current income consumed (C/
YH + YW) for each of our nine family types. In so doing we have chosen
the same demographic circumstances for all families: husbands and their
wives are assumed to be the same age; mothers are assumed to be age 22
when their first child is born; and couples are assumed to have a total of
three children, spaced two years apart.

The results of these simulations for selected parental ages are exhibited in table A.12. In the low and medium socioeconomic status (SES)
groups, husband's earnings rise to age 44, reach a maximum, and then
begin a gradual decline. For husbands in the high SES group, earnings
peak at age 49 and then decline. For working wives, earnings increase con-
tinuously with age, the steepness of the ascent being positively related to
education. Table A.12 shows substantial variation in family income (YH
+ YW) across the nine family types. At age 40, for example, pretax income ranges from $9,319 (in 1972–1973 dollars) in low SES families when
the wife does not work to $27,345 in high SES families where the wife
works full time for twelve months out of the year. Despite these wide differences in family income, however, there are much smaller variations in total
family consumption across family types. Again at age 40, annual family
spending ranges from a low of $10,838 to a high of $14,979. The smaller
range for consumption than for income is significant and important to re-
member. A large part of the explanation may be due to the progressive tax
structure in the United States and to differential savings rates across SES
groups. Whatever the reason, we find that, at age 40, our simulated high
SES families are spending on average between 60 and 65 percent of total
pretax income, whereas couples in low SES families spend nearly all of
(and in some instances more than) their income. The practical implication
of this leveling of consumption across a broad range of family incomes is a
corresponding leveling of estimated parental expenditures on children
when the same variation in family incomes is considered. Therefore, it may
be the case that the largest impact of children on a family's finances is in
terms of reducing long-term net worth in families from low SES back-
grounds. In other words, high and low SES families may not be differentiated so much by how much they spend as by how much they save, that is,
by accumulated net worth.

## Patterns of Family Consumption Spending

Since one of our interests concerning parental expenditures on children will be with how total expenditures at a given age are distributed

TABLE A.12 Simulated Values for Earnings, Income, and Consumption by Family Type and Selected Ages of Family Head

| Parental Age and Item Simulated | Family Type[a] | | | | | | | | |
|---|---|---|---|---|---|---|---|---|---|
| | Low SES | | | Medium SES | | | High SES | | |
| | No work | Part time | Full time | No work | Part time | Full time | No work | Part time | Full time |
| **25** | | | | | | | | | |
| YH[b] | $7,285 | $7,285 | $7,285 | $8,782 | $8,782 | $8,782 | $9,389 | $9,389 | $9,389 |
| YW[c] | 0 | 1,578 | 5,737 | 0 | 1,962 | 6,122 | 0 | 3,231 | 7,391 |
| YH+YW | 7,285 | 8,863 | 13,022 | 8,782 | 10,745 | 14,905 | 9,389 | 12,620 | 16,779 |
| C[d] | 7,459 | 8,102 | 9,797 | 7,921 | 8,653 | 10,205 | 8,108 | 9,268 | 10,762 |
| C/YH+YW | 1.024 | 0.914 | 0.752 | 0.902 | 0.805 | 0.685 | 0.864 | 0.734 | 0.641 |
| **30** | | | | | | | | | |
| YH | 8,267 | 8,267 | 8,267 | 10,328 | 10,328 | 10,328 | 13,533 | 13,533 | 13,533 |
| YW | 0 | 1,602 | 5,762 | 0 | 2,064 | 6,224 | 0 | 3,586 | 7,746 |
| YH+YW | 8,267 | 9,869 | 14,029 | 10,328 | 12,392 | 16,551 | 13,533 | 17,119 | 21,279 |
| C | 7,762 | 8,379 | 9,980 | 8,398 | 9,094 | 10,498 | 9,386 | 10,332 | 11,430 |
| C/YH+YW | 0.939 | 0.849 | 0.711 | 0.813 | 0.734 | 0.634 | 0.694 | 0.604 | 0.537 |
| **35** | | | | | | | | | |
| YH | 8,945 | 8,945 | 8,945 | 11,401 | 11,401 | 11,401 | 16,699 | 16,699 | 16,699 |
| YW | 0 | 1,627 | 5,786 | 0 | 2,165 | 6,325 | 0 | 3,941 | 8,101 |
| YH+YW | 8,945 | 10,571 | 14,731 | 11,401 | 13,566 | 17,726 | 16,699 | 20,641 | 24,800 |
| C | 8,745 | 9,346 | 10,882 | 9,502 | 10,180 | 11,481 | 11,136 | 11,889 | 12,684 |
| C/YH+YW | 0.978 | 0.884 | 0.739 | 0.834 | 0.750 | 0.648 | 0.667 | 0.576 | 0.511 |
| **40** | | | | | | | | | |
| YH | 9,319 | 9,319 | 9,319 | 12,001 | 12,001 | 12,001 | 18,888 | 18,888 | 18,888 |
| YW | 0 | 1,651 | 5,811 | 0 | 2,267 | 6,426 | 0 | 4,296 | 8,456 |
| YH+YW | 9,319 | 10,970 | 15,130 | 12,001 | 14,268 | 18,427 | 18,888 | 23,185 | 27,345 |
| C | 10,838 | 11,434 | 12,934 | 11,665 | 12,343 | 13,587 | 13,789 | 14,394 | 14,979 |
| C/YH+YW | 1.163 | 1.042 | 0.855 | 0.972 | 0.865 | 0.737 | 0.730 | 0.621 | 0.548 |
| **45** | | | | | | | | | |
| YH | 9,389 | 9,389 | 9,389 | 12,129 | 12,129 | 12,129 | 20,100 | 20,100 | 20,100 |
| YW | 0 | 1,676 | 5,835 | 0 | 2,368 | 6,528 | 0 | 4,652 | 8,811 |
| YH+YW | 9,389 | 11,065 | 15,224 | 12,129 | 14,497 | 18,657 | 20,100 | 24,752 | 28,911 |
| C | 13,190 | 13,792 | 15,285 | 14,035 | 14,736 | 15,968 | 16,492 | 17,017 | 17,487 |
| C/YH+YW | 1.404 | 1.246 | 1.004 | 1.157 | 1.016 | 0.856 | 0.821 | 0.688 | 0.605 |

a. In these simulations children are assumed to be household members until age 25.
b. Predicted husband's earnings.
c. Predicted wife's earnings.
d. Predicted total family current consumption expenditures.

across major consumption categories, we first must inquire how the family unit as a whole divides total family consumption among competing groups of goods and services. The major groups on which we focus are food at home, food away from home, shelter (excluding payments on mortgage principal, which are treated separately as a reduction in liabilities), fuel and utilities, household goods, clothing, transportation, health care, recreation, and miscellaneous expenditures (comprising alcohol, tobacco, personal care, reading, private education, public education, and other miscellaneous items). Total food consumption may be treated as the sum of food at home and food away from home. Total housing is the aggregation of shelter, fuel and utilities, and household goods and operations.

We are interested in estimating "a set" of Engel functions, one for each category of consumption, that describes the dependence of expenditures on the $i$th commodity group on total family spending as well as on family size and composition. There are many ways to do this. A variety of functional forms is given in Prais and Houthakker (1955). More recent work has aimed at incorporating demographic variables in linear expenditure systems (see, for example, Muellbauer 1974, 1975, 1977a, 1977b; Pollak and Wales 1978a, 1978b, 1978c, 1980a, 1980b). For our purposes a relatively straightforward specification will suffice. We have chosen to estimate

$E_i = f(C, C^2, AGES(1), \ldots, AGES(12))$, where
$E_i$ = family expenditures on the $i$th expenditure category,
$C$ = total family consumption expenditures, and
$AGES(j)$ = the number of full-year equivalent family members in the $j$th age group, $j = 1, 2, \ldots, 12$.

As a reminder to the reader, the twelve age groups are under 1, 1–2, 3–5, 6–8, 9–11, 12–14, 15–17, 18–24, 25–34, 35–44, 45–54, and 55 and over.

The reason for specifying the same functional form for each expenditure category is to solve the adding-up problem (see Espenshade 1973: 33–33 and 82–84). We want to guarantee that the predicted values for food at home, food away from home, and so on, for given values of C, $C^2$ and $AGES(i)$, $i = 1 \ldots, 12$, will add up to C. If different specifications for each commodity group were used, this would not always be the case.

Our estimated equations for allocating total family spending across the ten categories of consumption are shown in table A.13. Spending on a particular category is in all instances positively related to total family spending (C) and, with the exception of shelter, negatively related to $C^2$. It is difficult to generalize about the effect of family size and composition, though the increase in health care expenditures for household members over age 45 is especially evident.

To show the implications of equations in table A.13, we have selected two age groups from the simulations in table A.12 (ages 30 and 40) and, for each of the nine family types, disaggregated total family spending into its ten constituent parts. The results are displayed in table A.14. The most prominent categories of consumption in the family's total budget are food at home, shelter, and transportation. Transportation expenditures take a relatively larger fraction of the budget when parents are age 40, partly because the three children are older (18, 16, and 14 years old) and have more activities requiring transportation.

## Variations in a Family's Level of Living

The reader will recall from our earlier discussion that we have elected to use as our measure of a family's material standard of living the percentage of total current consumption expenditure devoted to food consumed at home (PFDHM). Moreover, we are going to assume that two families that have the same value on PFDHM have the same standard or level of living,

TABLE A.13   Equations for Individual Categories of Consumption Spending: Total United States Dependent Variable (E2) = **Food at Home** (N = 8547)

| MODEL: EQ06 | | SSE | 40971212 | F RATIO | 387.15 |
|---|---|---|---|---|---|
| WEIGHT: WEIGHT | | DFE | 8532 | PROB>F | 0.0001 |
| DEP VAR: E2 | | MSE | 4802.064 | R-SQUARE | 0.3885 |

| Variable | DF | Parameter Estimate | Standard Error | T Ratio | PROB>\|T\| |
|---|---|---|---|---|---|
| INTERCEPT | 1 | −0.254115 | 0.044892 | −5.6606 | 0.0001 |
| C | 1 | 0.082209 | 0.002378947 | 34.5567 | 0.0001 |
| C2 | 1 | −0.000391648 | .00002541946 | −15.4074 | 0.0001 |
| AGES1 | 1 | 0.039905 | 0.042345 | 0.9424 | 0.3460 |
| AGES2 | 1 | 0.131756 | 0.024167 | 5.4520 | 0.0001 |
| AGES3 | 1 | 0.201229 | 0.019015 | 10.5824 | 0.0001 |
| AGES4 | 1 | 0.225902 | 0.017964 | 12.5750 | 0.0001 |
| AGES5 | 1 | 0.225707 | 0.016953 | 13.3136 | 0.0001 |
| AGES6 | 1 | 0.257254 | 0.017200 | 14.9566 | 0.0001 |
| AGES7 | 1 | 0.251283 | 0.018356 | 13.6891 | 0.0001 |
| AGES8 | 1 | 0.143103 | 0.017962 | 7.9671 | 0.0001 |
| AGES9 | 1 | 0.254106 | 0.025187 | 10.0888 | 0.0001 |
| AGES10 | 1 | 0.417898 | 0.024998 | 16.7174 | 0.0001 |
| AGES11 | 1 | 0.477124 | 0.022471 | 21.2328 | 0.0001 |
| AGES12 | 1 | 0.524256 | 0.028081 | 18.6697 | 0.0001 |

TABLE A.13 Equations for Individual Categories of Consumption Spending:
(*continued*) Total United States Dependent Variable (E3) = **Food Away from Home** (N = 8547)

| MODEL: EQ06 | | SSE | 11159862 | F RATIO | 227.02 |
|---|---|---|---|---|---|
| WEIGHT: WEIGHT | | DFE | 8532 | PROB>F | 0.0001 |
| DEP VAR: E3 | | MSE | 1308.001 | R-SQUARE | 0.2714 |

| Variable | DF | Parameter Estimate | Standard Error | T Ratio | PROB>\|T\| |
|---|---|---|---|---|---|
| INTERCEPT | 1 | 0.021004 | 0.023429 | 0.8965 | 0.3700 |
| C | 1 | 0.061407 | 0.00124158 | 49.4584 | 0.0001 |
| C2 | 1 | −0.000279448 | 0.0000132665 | −21.0642 | 0.0001 |
| AGES1 | 1 | −0.061556 | 0.022100 | −2.7854 | 0.0054 |
| AGES2 | 1 | −0.075191 | 0.012613 | −5.9616 | 0.0001 |
| AGES3 | 1 | −0.059422 | 0.009924201 | −5.9876 | 0.0001 |
| AGES4 | 1 | −0.039309 | 0.009375644 | −4.1927 | 0.0001 |
| AGES5 | 1 | −0.020384 | 0.008847882 | −2.3039 | 0.0213 |
| AGES6 | 1 | −0.021702 | 0.008976784 | −2.4175 | 0.0156 |
| AGES7 | 1 | 0.00971785 | 0.009580295 | 1.0144 | 0.3104 |
| AGES8 | 1 | −0.039865 | 0.009374256 | −4.2527 | 0.0001 |
| AGES9 | 1 | −0.018923 | 0.013145 | −1.4395 | 0.1500 |
| AGES10 | 1 | −0.017917 | 0.013046 | −1.3733 | 0.1697 |
| AGES11 | 1 | −0.046439 | 0.011728 | −3.9598 | 0.0001 |
| AGES12 | 1 | −0.043264 | 0.014655 | −2.9521 | 0.0032 |

TABLE A.13 Equations for Individual Categories of Consumption Spending:
(*continued*) Total United States Dependent Variable (E5) = **Shelter** (N = 8547)

| MODEL: EQ06 | | SSE | 79671720 | F RATIO | 1833.47 |
|---|---|---|---|---|---|
| WEIGHT: WEIGHT | | DFE | 8532 | PROB>F | 0.0001 |
| DEP VAR: E5 | | MSE | 9337.989 | R-SQUARE | 0.7505 |

| Variable | DF | Parameter Estimate | Standard Error | T Ratio | PROB>\|T\| |
|---|---|---|---|---|---|
| INTERCEPT | 1 | 1.407827 | 0.062601 | 22.4888 | 0.0001 |
| C | 1 | 0.036505 | 0.003317397 | 11.0040 | 0.0001 |
| C2 | 1 | 0.004014187 | .00003544697 | 113.2449 | 0.0001 |
| AGES1 | 1 | 0.115176 | 0.059049 | 1.9505 | 0.0511 |
| AGES2 | 1 | 0.089369 | 0.033700 | 2.6519 | 0.0080 |
| AGES3 | 1 | −0.024831 | 0.026517 | −0.9364 | 0.3491 |
| AGES4 | 1 | −0.059325 | 0.025051 | −2.3682 | 0.0179 |
| AGES5 | 1 | −0.066183 | 0.023641 | −2.7995 | 0.0051 |
| AGES6 | 1 | −0.058004 | 0.023985 | −2.4183 | 0.0156 |
| AGES7 | 1 | −0.102250 | 0.025598 | −3.9945 | 0.0001 |
| AGES8 | 1 | −0.193302 | 0.025047 | −7.7175 | 0.0001 |
| AGES9 | 1 | −0.192539 | 0.035123 | −5.4819 | 0.0001 |
| AGES10 | 1 | −0.335817 | 0.034859 | −9.6336 | 0.0001 |
| AGES11 | 1 | −0.387217 | 0.031336 | −12.3571 | 0.0001 |
| AGES12 | 1 | −0.488414 | 0.039158 | −12.4730 | 0.0001 |

TABLE A.13    Equations for Individual Categories of Consumption Spending:
(*continued*)    Total United States Dependent Variable (E6) = **Fuel and Utilities**
(N = 8547)

| MODEL: EQ06 | | SSE | 3559866 | F RATIO | 213.87 |
|---|---|---|---|---|---|
| WEIGHT: WEIGHT | | DFE | 8532 | PROB>F | 0.0001 |
| DEP VAR: E6 | | MSE | 417.236943 | R-SQUARE | 0.2598 |

| Variable | DF | Parameter Estimate | Standard Error | T Ratio | PROB > \|T\| |
|---|---|---|---|---|---|
| INTERCEPT | 1 | 0.063673 | 0.013233 | 4.8118 | 0.0001 |
| C | 1 | 0.023121 | 0.0007012327 | 32.9718 | 0.0001 |
| C2 | 1 | −0.000102955 | .00000749279 | −13.7406 | 0.0001 |
| AGES1 | 1 | 0.036367 | 0.012482 | 2.9136 | 0.0036 |
| AGES2 | 1 | 0.033065 | 0.007123505 | 4.6417 | 0.0001 |
| AGES3 | 1 | 0.037081 | 0.005605094 | 6.6156 | 0.0001 |
| AGES4 | 1 | 0.042632 | 0.005295275 | 8.0510 | 0.0001 |
| AGES5 | 1 | 0.035714 | 0.0049972 | 7.1467 | 0.0001 |
| AGES6 | 1 | 0.027806 | 0.005070002 | 5.4843 | 0.0001 |
| AGES7 | 1 | 0.026229 | 0.005410859 | 4.8475 | 0.0001 |
| AGES8 | 1 | 0.004616062 | 0.005294491 | 0.8719 | 0.3833 |
| AGES9 | 1 | 0.062422 | 0.007424238 | 8.4079 | 0.0001 |
| AGES10 | 1 | 0.095152 | 0.007368498 | 12.9134 | 0.0001 |
| AGES11 | 1 | 0.109211 | 0.006623715 | 16.4879 | 0.0001 |
| AGES12 | 1 | 0.109878 | 0.008277178 | 13.2748 | 0.0001 |

TABLE A.13    Equations for Individual Categories of Consumption Spending:
(*continued*)    Total United States Dependent Variable (E7) = **Household
Goods** (N = 8547)

| MODEL: EQ06 | | SSE | 29182003 | F RATIO | 339.54 |
|---|---|---|---|---|---|
| WEIGHT: WEIGHT | | DFE | 8532 | PROB>F | 0.0001 |
| DEP VAR: E7 | | MSE | 3420.3 | R-SQUARE | 0.3578 |

| Variable | DF | Parameter Estimate | Standard Error | T Ratio | PROB > \|T\| |
|---|---|---|---|---|---|
| INTERCEPT | 1 | 0.098601 | 0.037887 | 2.6025 | 0.0093 |
| C | 1 | 0.126883 | 0.002007719 | 63.1975 | 0.0001 |
| C2 | 1 | −0.000524875 | .00002145283 | −24.4665 | 0.0001 |
| AGES1 | 1 | 0.090924 | 0.035737 | 2.5442 | 0.0110 |
| AGES2 | 1 | 0.121878 | 0.020396 | 5.9757 | 0.0001 |
| AGES3 | 1 | 0.051016 | 0.016048 | 3.1789 | 0.0015 |
| AGES4 | 1 | −0.023433 | 0.015161 | −1.5456 | 0.1222 |
| AGES5 | 1 | −0.027360 | 0.014308 | −1.9123 | 0.0559 |
| AGES6 | 1 | −0.074892 | 0.014516 | −5.1592 | 0.0001 |
| AGES7 | 1 | −0.110792 | 0.015492 | −7.1516 | 0.0001 |
| AGES8 | 1 | −0.213278 | 0.015159 | −14.0696 | 0.0001 |
| AGES9 | 1 | −0.147971 | 0.021257 | −6.9612 | 0.0001 |
| AGES10 | 1 | −0.169970 | 0.021097 | −8.0566 | 0.0001 |
| AGES11 | 1 | −0.195368 | 0.018965 | −10.3017 | 0.0001 |
| AGES12 | 1 | −0.180995 | 0.023699 | −7.6373 | 0.0001 |

TABLE A.13 Equations for Individual Categories of Consumption Spending:
(*continued*) Total United States Dependent Variable (E8) = **Clothing**
(N = 8547)

| MODEL: EQ06 | | SSE | 15692610 | F RATIO | 467.48 |
|---|---|---|---|---|---|
| WEIGHT: WEIGHT | | DFE | 8532 | PROB>F | 0.0001 |
| DEP VAR: E8 | | MSE | 1839.265 | R-SQUARE | 0.4341 |

| Variable | DF | Parameter Estimate | Standard Error | T Ratio | PROB>\|T\| |
|---|---|---|---|---|---|
| INTERCEPT | 1 | −0.109353 | 0.027783 | −3.9360 | 0.0001 |
| C | 1 | 0.102350 | 0.001472289 | 69.5174 | 0.0001 |
| C2 | 1 | −0.000411618 | .00001573166 | −26.1650 | 0.0001 |
| AGES1 | 1 | −0.042312 | 0.026206 | −1.6146 | 0.1064 |
| AGES2 | 1 | −0.00146863 | 0.014956 | −0.0982 | 0.9218 |
| AGES3 | 1 | −0.012399 | 0.011768 | −1.0536 | 0.2921 |
| AGES4 | 1 | −0.00514396 | 0.011118 | −0.4627 | 0.6436 |
| AGES5 | 1 | −0.000496173 | 0.010492 | −0.0473 | 0.9623 |
| AGES6 | 1 | 0.062166 | 0.010645 | 5.8400 | 0.0001 |
| AGES7 | 1 | 0.044598 | 0.011360 | 3.9257 | 0.0001 |
| AGES8 | 1 | −0.0066668 | 0.011116 | −0.5997 | 0.5487 |
| AGES9 | 1 | −0.011453 | 0.015588 | −0.7348 | 0.4625 |
| AGES10 | 1 | −0.022846 | 0.015471 | −1.4767 | 0.1398 |
| AGES11 | 1 | −0.039407 | 0.013907 | −2.8336 | 0.0046 |
| AGES12 | 1 | −0.014357 | 0.017379 | −0.8261 | 0.4088 |

TABLE A.13 Equations for Individual Categories of Consumption Spending:
(*continued*) Total United States Dependent Variable (E9) = **Transportation**
(N = 8547)

| MODEL: EQ06 | | SSE | 145463517 | F RATIO | 396.59 |
|---|---|---|---|---|---|
| WEIGHT: WEIGHT | | DFE | 8532 | PROB>F | 0.0001 |
| DEP VAR: E9 | | MSE | 17049.17 | R-SQUARE | 0.3942 |

| Variable | DF | Parameter Estimate | Standard Error | T Ratio | PROB>\|T\| |
|---|---|---|---|---|---|
| INTERCEPT | 1 | −0.584113 | 0.084588 | −6.9054 | 0.0001 |
| C | 1 | 0.292910 | 0.004482522 | 65.3448 | 0.0001 |
| C2 | 1 | −0.00135814 | .00004789653 | −28.3557 | 0.0001 |
| AGES1 | 1 | −0.213497 | 0.079784 | −2.6758 | 0.0075 |
| AGES2 | 1 | −0.103761 | 0.045536 | −2.2787 | 0.0227 |
| AGES3 | 1 | −0.102479 | 0.035830 | −2.8602 | 0.0042 |
| AGES4 | 1 | −0.082479 | 0.033849 | −2.4367 | 0.0148 |
| AGES5 | 1 | −0.107829 | 0.031944 | −3.3756 | 0.0007 |
| AGES6 | 1 | −0.158317 | 0.032409 | −4.8849 | 0.0001 |
| AGES7 | 1 | −0.067956 | 0.034588 | −1.9647 | 0.0495 |
| AGES8 | 1 | 0.261598 | 0.033844 | 7.7295 | 0.0001 |
| AGES9 | 1 | −0.0058717 | 0.047458 | −0.1237 | 0.9015 |
| AGES10 | 1 | −0.036057 | 0.047102 | −0.7655 | 0.4440 |
| AGES11 | 1 | −0.057560 | 0.042341 | −1.3594 | 0.1740 |
| AGES12 | 1 | −0.054110 | 0.052911 | −1.0227 | 0.3065 |

TABLE A.13    Equations for Individual Categories of Consumption Spending:
(*continued*)     Total United States Dependent Variable (E10) = **Health Care**
(N = 8547)

| MODEL: EQ06 | | SSE | 20772030 | F RATIO | 119.17 |
|---|---|---|---|---|---|
| WEIGHT: WEIGHT | | DFE | 8532 | PROB>F | 0.0001 |
| DEP VAR: E10 | | MSE | 2434.603 | R-SQUARE | 0.1636 |

| Variable | DF | Parameter Estimate | Standard Error | T Ratio | PROB>\|T\| |
|---|---|---|---|---|---|
| INTERCEPT | 1 | −0.024661 | 0.031965 | −0.7715 | 0.4404 |
| C | 1 | 0.049131 | 0.001693889 | 29.0050 | 0.0001 |
| C2 | 1 | −.0000444342 | .00001809949 | −2.4550 | 0.0141 |
| AGES1 | 1 | 0.250966 | 0.030151 | 8.3237 | 0.0001 |
| AGES2 | 1 | −0.012794 | 0.017207 | −0.7435 | 0.4572 |
| AGES3 | 1 | 0.0009379963 | 0.013540 | 0.0693 | 0.9448 |
| AGES4 | 1 | −0.013098 | 0.012791 | −1.0240 | 0.3059 |
| AGES5 | 1 | −0.00243828 | 0.012071 | −0.2020 | 0.8399 |
| AGES6 | 1 | 0.013184 | 0.012247 | 1.0765 | 0.2817 |
| AGES7 | 1 | −0.000574764 | 0.013070 | −0.0440 | 0.9649 |
| AGES8 | 1 | −0.014632 | 0.012789 | −1.1441 | 0.2526 |
| AGES9 | 1 | 0.035883 | 0.017934 | 2.0008 | 0.0454 |
| AGES10 | 1 | 0.034315 | 0.017799 | 1.9279 | 0.0539 |
| AGES11 | 1 | 0.078068 | 0.016000 | 4.8792 | 0.0001 |
| AGES12 | 1 | 0.104138 | 0.019994 | 5.2084 | 0.0001 |

TABLE A.13    Equations for Individual Categories of Consumption Spending:
(*continued*)     Total United States Dependent Variable (E11) = **Recreation**
(N = 8547)

| MODEL: EQ06 | | SSE | 43530729 | F RATIO | 309.64 |
|---|---|---|---|---|---|
| WEIGHT: WEIGHT | | DFE | 8532 | PROB>F | 0.0001 |
| DEP VAR: E11 | | MSE | 5102.054 | R-SQUARE | 0.3369 |

| Variable | DF | Parameter Estimate | Standard Error | T Ratio | PROB>\|T\| |
|---|---|---|---|---|---|
| INTERCEPT | 1 | −0.061977 | 0.046273 | −1.3394 | 0.1805 |
| C | 1 | 0.146330 | 0.002452129 | 59.6749 | 0.0001 |
| C2 | 1 | −0.000619163 | .00002620143 | −23.6309 | 0.0001 |
| AGES1 | 1 | −0.167772 | 0.043647 | −3.8438 | 0.0001 |
| AGES2 | 1 | −0.104082 | 0.024910 | −4.1783 | 0.0001 |
| AGES3 | 1 | −0.073129 | 0.019600 | −3.7310 | 0.0002 |
| AGES4 | 1 | −0.057421 | 0.018517 | −3.1010 | 0.0019 |
| AGES5 | 1 | −0.015885 | 0.017475 | −0.9090 | 0.3634 |
| AGES6 | 1 | 0.002372637 | 0.017729 | 0.1338 | 0.8935 |
| AGES7 | 1 | −0.046163 | 0.018921 | −2.4397 | 0.0147 |
| AGES8 | 1 | −0.166606 | 0.018514 | −8.9988 | 0.0001 |
| AGES9 | 1 | −0.185573 | 0.025962 | −7.1480 | 0.0001 |
| AGES10 | 1 | −0.189884 | 0.025767 | −7.3693 | 0.0001 |
| AGES11 | 1 | −0.211159 | 0.023162 | −9.1165 | 0.0001 |
| AGES12 | 1 | −0.208607 | 0.028944 | −7.2072 | 0.0001 |

TABLE A.13 Equations for Individual Categories of Consumption Spending:
(*continued*) Total United States Dependent Variable (E12) = **Miscellaneous**
(N = 8547)

| MODEL: EQ06 | | SSE | 22663004 | F RATIO | 291.84 |
|---|---|---|---|---|---|
| WEIGHT: WEIGHT | | DFE | 8532 | PROB > F | 0.0001 |
| DEP VAR: E12 | | MSE | 2656.236 | R-SQUARE | 0.3238 |

| Variable | DF | Parameter Estimate | Standard Error | T Ratio | PROB > \|T\| |
|---|---|---|---|---|---|
| INTERCEPT | 1 | −0.556887 | 0.033388 | −16.6793 | 0.0001 |
| C | 1 | 0.079155 | 0.001769311 | 44.7380 | 0.0001 |
| C2 | 1 | −0.000281904 | .00001890539 | −14.9113 | 0.0001 |
| AGES1 | 1 | −0.048200 | 0.031493 | −1.5305 | 0.1259 |
| AGES2 | 1 | −0.078771 | 0.017974 | −4.3826 | 0.0001 |
| AGES3 | 1 | −0.018003 | 0.014142 | −1.2730 | 0.2031 |
| AGES4 | 1 | 0.011676 | 0.013361 | 0.8739 | 0.3822 |
| AGES5 | 1 | −0.020845 | 0.012609 | −1.6532 | 0.0983 |
| AGES6 | 1 | −0.049867 | 0.012792 | −3.8982 | 0.0001 |
| AGES7 | 1 | −0.00409282 | 0.013652 | −0.2998 | 0.7643 |
| AGES8 | 1 | 0.225032 | 0.013359 | 16.8453 | 0.0001 |
| AGES9 | 1 | 0.209920 | 0.018732 | 11.2062 | 0.0001 |
| AGES10 | 1 | 0.225126 | 0.018592 | 12.1089 | 0.0001 |
| AGES11 | 1 | 0.272747 | 0.016713 | 16.3198 | 0.0001 |
| AGES12 | 1 | 0.251474 | 0.020885 | 12.0412 | 0.0001 |

regardless of any other differences with respect to the volume of total consumption or to family size and/or composition.

The final task is therefore to examine the consumption-related and demographic determinants of variations in a family's level of living. Recall that earlier our estimated Engel equation for food at home (FDHM) was of the form

$$FDHM = f(\text{intercept}, C, C^2, AGES1, \ldots, AGES12).$$

Since this specification was assumed to be linear in the coefficients, we can divide both sides by C and write the new dependent variable as a percentage to yield

$$\frac{FDHM}{C} *100 = PFDHM = g\left(\text{intercept}, \frac{1}{C}, C, \frac{AGES1}{C}, \ldots, \frac{AGES12}{C}\right).$$

Some experimentation with stepwise regression procedures revealed the importance of per capita consumption (C/F, where F is total family size or the sum of AGES1, ..., AGES12) instead of C as a determinant of the percentage of total consumption devoted to food at home (PFDHM).

TABLE A.14  Simulated Patterns of Family Consumption Spending by Category of Consumption and by Family Type, CU Head Age 30 and 40 years
(*In thousands of dollars*)

| Parental Age and Item Simulated[a] | Family Type | | | | | | | | |
| --- | --- | --- | --- | --- | --- | --- | --- | --- | --- |
| | Low SES | | | Medium SES | | | High SES | | |
| | No work | Part time | Full time | No work | Part time | Full time | No work | Part time | Full time |
| **30** | | | | | | | | | |
| YH | 8.26672 | 8.26672 | 8.26672 | 10.32770 | 10.32770 | 10.32770 | 13.53274 | 13.53274 | 13.53274 |
| YW | 0.0 | 1.60221 | 5.76192 | 0.0 | 2.06391 | 6.22363 | 0.0 | 3.58620 | 7.74591 |
| YH+YW | 8.26672 | 9.86893 | 14.02865 | 10.32770 | 12.39161 | 16.55132 | 13.53274 | 17.11893 | 21.27864 |
| C | 7.76221 | 8.37893 | 9.98008 | 8.39769 | 9.09434 | 10.49841 | 9.38592 | 10.33218 | 11.42978 |
| FDHCF | 1.52159 | 1.56839 | 1.68849 | 1.56981 | 1.62230 | 1.72694 | 1.64416 | 1.71463 | 1.79550 |
| FDACF | 0.30493 | 0.34002 | 0.43013 | 0.34109 | 0.38046 | 0.45899 | 0.39686 | 0.44975 | 0.51048 |
| SHLCF | 1.40449 | 1.46696 | 1.64341 | 1.46891 | 1.54325 | 1.70494 | 1.57553 | 1.68497 | 1.82092 |
| FTLCF | 0.48413 | 0.49736 | 0.53136 | 0.49776 | 0.51262 | 0.54225 | 0.51880 | 0.53876 | 0.56168 |
| HGDCF | 0.76008 | 0.83310 | 1.02083 | 0.83532 | 0.91731 | 1.08103 | 0.95148 | 1.06175 | 1.18848 |
| CLOCF | 0.61472 | 0.67374 | 0.82552 | 0.67553 | 0.74182 | 0.87420 | 0.76944 | 0.85861 | 0.96112 |
| TRSCF | 1.32850 | 1.49563 | 1.92470 | 1.50069 | 1.68820 | 2.06211 | 1.76629 | 2.01812 | 2.30717 |
| HELCF | 0.40053 | 0.43039 | 0.50775 | 0.43130 | 0.46499 | 0.53275 | 0.47907 | 0.52473 | 0.57760 |
| RECCF | 0.47744 | 0.56152 | 0.77762 | 0.56407 | 0.65847 | 0.84689 | 0.69780 | 0.82471 | 0.97054 |
| MISCF | 0.46573 | 0.51174 | 0.63020 | 0.51314 | 0.56485 | 0.66823 | 0.58641 | 0.65605 | 0.73620 |
| C/YH+YW | 0.93897 | 0.84902 | 0.71141 | 0.81312 | 0.73391 | 0.63429 | 0.69357 | 0.60355 | 0.53715 |

TABLE A.14 (continued)  Simulated Patterns of Family Consumption Spending by Category of Consumption and by Family Type, CU Head Age 30 and 40 years
(*In thousands of dollars*)

| Parental Age and Item Simulated[a] | Low SES | | | Medium SES | | | High SES | | |
|---|---|---|---|---|---|---|---|---|---|
| | No work | Part time | Full time | No work | Part time | Full time | No work | Part time | Full time |
| **40** | | | | | | | | | |
| YH | 9.31878 | 9.31878 | 9.31878 | 12.00098 | 12.00098 | 12.00098 | 18.88841 | 18.88841 | 18.88841 |
| YW | 0.0 | 1.65115 | 5.81036 | 0.0 | 2.26675 | 6.42647 | 0.0 | 4.29647 | 8.45618 |
| YH+YW | 9.31878 | 10.96993 | 15.12965 | 12.00098 | 14.26773 | 18.42744 | 18.88841 | 23.18488 | 27.34459 |
| C | 10.83814 | 11.43376 | 12.93431 | 11.66516 | 12.34309 | 13.58716 | 13.78881 | 14.39353 | 14.97899 |
| FDHCF | 2.07822 | 2.12198 | 2.23101 | 2.13891 | 2.18826 | 2.27789 | 2.29231 | 2.33534 | 2.37673 |
| FDACF | 0.56603 | 0.59890 | 0.68083 | 0.61162 | 0.64870 | 0.71608 | 0.72692 | 0.75929 | 0.79044 |
| SHLCF | 1.24981 | 1.32480 | 1.52636 | 1.35471 | 1.44479 | 1.61970 | 1.64922 | 1.73970 | 1.83011 |
| FTLCF | 0.55112 | 0.56353 | 0.59446 | 0.56833 | 0.58233 | 0.60777 | 0.61186 | 0.62409 | 0.63586 |
| HGDCF | 0.67322 | 0.74183 | 1.91303 | 0.76838 | 0.84586 | 0.98678 | 1.00947 | 1.07725 | 1.14251 |
| CLOCF | 1.00598 | 1.06148 | 1.20001 | 1.08297 | 1.14565 | 1.25971 | 1.27807 | 1.33295 | 1.38579 |
| TRSCF | 2.39416 | 2.55061 | 2.94047 | 2.61113 | 2.78759 | 3.10818 | 3.15975 | 3.31373 | 3.46187 |
| HELCF | 0.56922 | 0.59789 | 0.66999 | 0.60902 | 0.64160 | 0.70129 | 0.71096 | 0.73991 | 0.76791 |
| RECCF | 0.86107 | 0.94001 | 1.13695 | 0.97057 | 1.05969 | 1.22176 | 1.24785 | 1.32579 | 1.40081 |
| MISCF | 0.88922 | 0.93262 | 1.04109 | 0.94943 | 0.99851 | 1.08789 | 1.10229 | 1.14535 | 1.18685 |
| C/YH+YW | 1.16304 | 1.04228 | 0.85490 | 0.97202 | 0.86511 | 0.73733 | 0.73001 | 0.62082 | 0.54779 |

a. FDHCF = Food at home    FDACF = Food away from home    SHLCF = Shelter    FTLCF = Fuel and utilities
HGDCF = Household goods    CLOCF = Clothing    TRSCF = Transportation
HELCF = Health care    RECCF = Recreation    MISCF = Miscellaneous

TABLE A.15   Standard-of-living Equation: Total United States (N = 8547)

| MODEL: REG4 | | SSE | 4087456012 | F RATIO | 293.10 |
|---|---|---|---|---|---|
| WEIGHT: WEIGHT | | DFE | 8532 | PROB>F | 0.0001 |
| DEP VAR: PFDHM | | MSE | 479073.6 | R-SQUARE | 0.3248 |

| Variable | DF | Parameter Estimate | Standard Error | T Ratio | PROB > \|T\| |
|---|---|---|---|---|---|
| INTERCEPT | 1 | 15.137632 | 0.415916 | 36.3959 | 0.0001 |
| FC | 1 | 5.672838 | 1.016080 | 5.5831 | 0.0001 |
| CF | 1 | −1.157694 | 0.071141 | −16.2732 | 0.0001 |
| AGESFC1 | 1 | −2.942638 | 0.377048 | −7.8044 | 0.0001 |
| AGESFC2 | 1 | −1.368563 | 0.314735 | −4.3483 | 0.0001 |
| AGESFC3 | 1 | −0.112245 | 0.267261 | −0.4200 | 0.6745 |
| AGESFC4 | 1 | 0.065775 | 0.251609 | 0.2614 | 0.7938 |
| AGESFC5 | 1 | 0.018521 | 0.248541 | 0.0745 | 0.9406 |
| AGESFC6 | 1 | 0.308798 | 0.259031 | 1.1921 | 0.2332 |
| AGESFC7 | 1 | −1.001202 | 0.295434 | −3.3889 | 0.0007 |
| AGESFC8 | 1 | −1.927143 | 0.311819 | −6.1803 | 0.0001 |
| AGESFC9 | 1 | 1.602884 | 0.457486 | 3.5037 | 0.0005 |
| AGESFC10 | 1 | 5.193213 | 0.464314 | 11.1847 | 0.0001 |
| AGESFC11 | 1 | 7.607865 | 0.430428 | 17.6751 | 0.0001 |
| AGESFC12 | 1 | 7.598879 | 0.569068 | 13.3532 | 0.0001 |

Therefore, substituting C/F for C in the above equation yields the final specification for PFDHM:

$$PFDHM = h\left(intercept, \frac{F}{C}, \frac{C}{F}, \frac{AGES1*F}{C}, \ldots, \frac{AGES12*F}{C}\right).$$

This relation, estimated on the basis of all 8,547 observations, is exhibited in table A.15. We define this estimated regression as our standard-of-living (SOL) equation, and we use it to make standard-of-living comparisons among diverse family types.

# Notes

1. A companion study of opportunity expenditures on American children is currently underway at The Urban Institute.

2. The interested reader may consult Espenshade (1977) for a survey of the literature on the value of children.

3. The ability of the absent parent to pay child support is discussed in Judith Cassetty's (1978) book, *Child Support and Public Policy*. Using data from child support cases in Michigan, she finds that lower-income fathers pay a much larger percentage of their incomes in child support than higher-income fathers. The range as a percentage of the absent father's net income was from 11 to 33. Lenore Weitzman (1982) discovered the same propensity in California. In her 1978 interview sample, men with net after tax incomes under $10,000 were ordered to pay 37 percent of their net income in child support, and those with incomes between $10,000 and $30,000 were ordered to pay 25 percent. Men with incomes over $50,000 net were ordered to pay only 5 percent in child support. Weitzman (1982) reports, "The pattern that emerges from these data is that a man is rarely ordered to part with more than a third of his net income, no matter what his income level" (p. 4048), despite the fact that judges and attorneys who were interviewed often referred to an informal limit of one-half. Moreover, even though child support schedules exist in California for the purposes of setting temporary awards and close to 60 percent of the Los Angeles judges Weitzman (1982) interviewed said they consistently relied on these schedules, the amounts of support awarded were lower than the amounts in the schedules judges use to set temporary orders.

4. Criteria used by other states in determining child support payments are reviewed by Cassetty (1978). In each of the seven states she examines, current earned income is used as the underlying measure of the ability of the absent parent to pay child support, but the standards differ as to the measure of economic well-being that is used to determine the amount of income available for child support and, also, how much of the available income is then applied to child support. For related information, see Freed and Foster (1981) and Sauber and Taittonen (1977).

5. Personal communication, August 1, 1983.

6. Personal communication, July 29, 1983.

NOTE TO CHAPTER 2

1. Jean L. Pennock, "Cost of Raising a Child," 47th Annual Agricultural Outlook Conference, U.S. Department of Agriculture, Consumer and Food Economics Research Division (February 18, 1970) and "Cost of Raising a Child," U.S. Department of Agriculture, Agricultural Research Service, Consumer and Food Economics Research Division, CFE (Adm.)—318, September 1971.

NOTES TO CHAPTER 3

1. U.S. Bureau of Labor Statistics, Division of Living Conditions Studies, Washington, D.C. 20212.
2. Material standard of living is assumed to exclude the utility derived from children.
3. Additional examples of the application of this method are contained in Espenshade (1973).

NOTES TO CHAPTER 4

1. The only exception was the equation for black husbands' earnings. Since education was a statistically insignificant predictor, the equation was estimated on age, age squared, and interactions with occupation only. As a consequence, black husbands' earnings will be identical for low and medium SES groups.
2. U.S. Department of Health and Human Services, National Center for Health Statistics, *Health, United States, 1981*, table 74.
3. Roberta Barnes and Robert Moffitt. 1982. "A Dynamic Model of the Expectations and Fertility of Childless Women." Final Report on NICHD Contract no. N01-HD-12827. Barnes and Moffitt examine effects of first children being born when the mother is, alternatively, 20–24, 25–29, and 30–34 years old. We chose the midpoints of these age intervals for our estimates.
4. The inflation rate was calculated from CPI data for 1960, 1961, 1972, and 1973. See U.S. Bureau of the Census (1979), table no. 790.
5. Per capita personal consumption expenditure, expressed in constant 1972 dollars, rose from $2,507 in 1960 to $3,648 in 1973. See U.S. Bureau of the Census (1979), table no. 719.
6. See, for example, Mork (1966), Pennock (1970a, 1970b) and U.S. Department of Agriculture (1971).
7. U.S. Department of Agriculture (1982).
8. CPI data for 1981 are taken from U.S. Department of Labor, *Monthly Labor Review* (November 1982), table 17.
9. Net saving is that part of total family saving that is occasioned by or is on behalf of the child; it may be positive or negative (Espenshade 1973: 41).
10. Edwards (1981) concludes that per child costs in five-child families average from 20 to 24 percent below those in two-child families. Average expenditures per child decline between 7 and 12 percent in going from two to three children and by the same amount in going from three to four. Expenditures per child between four- and five-child families decrease only 4 or 5 percent.
11. A comprehensive methodological critique of the USDA's procedures is beyond the scope of this work. Part of this critique is already available in Espenshade (1973, 12–19). Our comments here are directed to a more recent documentation prepared by Edwards (1981).
12. It bears repeating that both we and the USDA are measuring living standards in

terms of current consumption data. If durables were included, a different conclusion might emerge regarding life-cycle changes in family levels of living.

13. For urban and rural nonfarm children, one may interpret the USDA estimates as average expenditures per child in families with not more than five children. Table 5 in Edwards (1981) contains a series of adjustment factors that can be applied to the basic estimates to compute average expenditures on children in families with a specific number of children (two, three, four, or five). But it is not clear how these adjustments could be used to infer marginal expenditure estimates.

14. Masnick and Bane (1980, chap. 3).

15. "How to project your child's college cost." *Business Week*, January 24, 1977, p. 74.

#### NOTES TO THE APPENDIX

1. Current consumption expenses, excluding personal insurance, gifts and contributions refer to the transaction cost of goods and services acquired during the interview period for consumption within the consumer unit. Estimates include both excise and sales taxes and exclude purchases or portions of purchases directly assignable to business purposes. Also excluded are periodic credit or installment payments on goods or services already acquired. The full cost of each purchase was recorded even though full payment may not have been made at the date of purchase. The unpaid portion of such a transaction is included as an increase in liabilities.

2. $AGES(i) = MALAGE(i) + FEMAGE(i)$, $i = 1, 2, \ldots, 12$.

# References

Arnold, Fred and James T. Fawcett. 1976. *The value of children: A cross-national study, vol. 3: Hawaii.* Honolulu: East-West Population Institute, East-West Center.

Behrman, Jere R., Robert A. Pollak, and Paul Taubman. 1982. "Parental preferences and provisions for progeny." *Journal of Political Economy* 90 (February): 52–73.

Bentley, Jerome T., Charles Ofori-Mensa, Michael R. Ransom, and Donald E. Wise. 1981. The cost of children: A household expenditures approach. Final Report to National Institute of Child Health and Human Development under contract No. NO1-HD-92823.

*Business Week.* 1977. "How to project your child's college cost." January 24, p. 74.

Cassetty, Judith. 1978. *Child support and public policy: Securing support from absent parents.* Lexington, Mass.: D.C. Heath.

Chambers, David L. 1979. *Making fathers pay: The enforcement of child support.* Chicago: University of Chicago Press.

College Entrance Examination Board. 1981. *The college cost book 1981–1982.* Second Edition. New York: College Entrance Examination Board.

Dublin, Louis I., and Alfred J. Lotka. 1946. *The money value of a man.* Revised Edition. New York: The Ronald Press Company.

Edwards, Carolyn S. 1981. "USDA estimates of the cost of raising a child: A guide to their use and interpretation." U.S. Department of Agriculture, Miscellaneous Publication 1411.

Engel, Ernst. 1883. Der Kostenwert des Menschen, Volkswirtsch Zeitfragen H. 37/38, Berlin.

——————. 1887. Consumption, Bulletin de l'Institut de Statistique II, 1, Rome.

——————. 1895. *Die Liebenskasten Belgischer Arbeit Familien Fruker und Jetzt—Ermittelt Aus Familienhaushaltrechnungen.* Bul. Institut. Internatl. Statis. 9.

121

*References*

Espenshade, Thomas J. 1972. "The price of children and socio-economic theories of fertility." *Population Studies* 26 (July): 207–221.
————. 1973. *The cost of children in urban United States.* Berkeley, California: Institute of International Studies Population Monograph Series no. 14, University of California.
————. 1977. "The value and cost of children." *Population Bulletin* 32 (April).
————. 1980. "Raising a child can now cost $85,000." *Intercom* 8 (September).
"Estimating Equivalent Incomes or Budget Costs by Family Type." 1960. *Monthly Labor Review* 83 (November): 1197–1200.
Freed, Doris Jonas, and Henry H. Foster, Jr. 1981. Divorce in the fifty states: An overview. *Family Law Quarterly* 14, no. 4 (Winter): 229–284.
Henderson, A. M. 1949–1950. "The cost of children." *Population Studies* Part I 3(2) (September 1949): 130–150; Parts II and III 4(3) (December 1950): 267–298.
Jacobs, Eva. 1977. "Changes in the distribution of consumer spending." *Monthly Labor Review* 100 (September): 33–34.
Lauderdale, Michael, Rosalie Anderson, and Jay Spiegel. 1981. *Family foster care reimbursement: Results of a national survey conducted by region VI adoptive resource center.* Center for Social Work Research, School of Social Work, University of Texas at Austin.
Lazear, Edward P., and Robert T. Michael. 1980. "Family size and the distribution of real per capita income." *American Economic Review* 70 (March): 91–107.
Lillydahl, Jane H., and Larry D. Sindell. 1982. "The scope of the grants economy and income distribution: An examination of intergenerational transfers of income." *American Journal of Economics and Sociology* 41 (April): 125–139.
Lindert, Peter. 1978. *Fertility and scarcity in America.* Princeton: Princeton University Press.
Masnick, George, and Mary Jo Bane. 1980. *The nation's families: 1960–1990.* Cambridge, Massachusetts: Joint Center for Urban Studies of MIT and Harvard University.
Moon, Marilyn, and Eugene Smolensky. 1977. "Income, economic status, and policy toward the aged." In *Income support policies for the aged.* G. S. Tolley and Richard V. Burkhauser, eds., 45–60. Cambridge, Massachusetts: Ballinger Publishing Company.
Morgan, James N. 1978. "Intra-family transfers revisited: The support of dependents inside the family." In *Five Thousand American Families—Patterns of Economic Progress.* Greg J. Duncan and James N. Morgan, eds., 347, 365. Ann Arbor, Michigan: Institute for Social Research.
Mork, Lucile F. 1966. "Cost of raising a child." 44th Annual Agricultural Outlook Conference, U.S. Department of Agriculture, Consumer and Food Economics Research Division (November 15).
Muellbauer, John. 1974. "Household composition, Engel curves and welfare comparisons between households." *European Economic Review* 5: 103–22.
————. 1975. "Identification and consumer unit scales." *Econometrica* 43: 807–09.
————. 1977a. "Testing the Barten model of household composition effects and the cost of children." *Economic Journal* 87: 460–87.
————. 1977b. "The estimation of the Prais-Houthakker model of equivalence scales." London: Birkbeck College, Department of Economics. Discussion Paper no. 52.

Nicholson, J. L. 1949. "Variations in working class family expenditure." *Journal of the Royal Statistical Society* 112 (Pt. IV): 359-411.

Ogburn, William F. 1919. "The financial cost of rearing a child." In *Standards of child welfare*, 26-30. U.S. Department of Labor Children's Bureau Conference Series no. 1, Publication no. 60.

Olson, Lawrence. 1982. Expenditures on children. Final Report to NICHD under contract no. NO1-HD-92825.

Orshansky, Mollie. 1965a. "Counting the poor: Another look at the poverty profile." *Social Security Bulletin* 28 (January): 3-29.

————. 1965b. "Who's who among the poor: A demographic view of poverty." *Social Security Bulletin* 28 (July): 3-32.

————. 1969. "How poverty is measured." *Monthly Labor Review* 92: 37-41.

Pennock, Jean L. 1970a. "Cost of raising a child." 47th Annual Agricultural Outlook Conference, U.S. Department of Agriculture, Consumer and Food Economics Research Division (February 18).

————. 1970b. "Cost of raising a child." *Family Economics Review* (March): 13-17.

Pollak, Robert, and Terrence Wales. 1978a. "Comparison of the quadratic expenditure system and translog demand systems with alternative specifications of demographic effects." Vancouver: University of British Columbia. Department of Economics. Discussion Paper no. 78-21.

————. 1978b. "Estimation of complete demand systems from household budget data: The linear and quadratic expenditure systems." *American Economic Review* 68: 348-59.

————. 1978c. "Welfare comparisons and equivalence scales." Philadelphia: University of Pennsylvania, July.

————. 1980a. "Comparison of the quadratic expenditure system and translog demand systems with alternative specifications of demographic effects." *Econometrica* 48 (April): 595-612.

————. 1980b. "Demographic variables in demand analysis." Vancouver: University of British Columbia, Department of Economics. Discussion Paper no. 78-48.

Prais, S., and H. Houthakker. 1955. *The analysis of family budgets*. Cambridge: Cambridge University Press.

Reed, Ritchie H., and Susan McIntosh. 1972. "Costs of children," In vol. 2, *Economic Aspects of Population Change*. Commission on Population Growth and the American Future. Washington, D.C.: U.S. Government Printing Office.

Sauber, Mignon, and Edith Taittonen. 1977. *Guide for determining the ability of an absent parent to pay child support*. Research and Program Planning Information Department, Community Council of Greater New York.

Sheshinski, Eytan, and Yoram Weiss. 1982. "Inequality within and between families." *Journal of Political Economy* 90 (February): 105-127.

Sohn, Sara A. 1970. *The cost of raising a child*. New York: Institute of Life Insurance, Division of Statistics and Research.

Turchi, Boone A. 1975. *The demand for children: The economics of fertility in the United States*. Cambridge, Massachusetts: Ballinger Publishing Company.

————. 1979. "The monetary cost of a child: A methodology and new estimates." Unpublished manuscript. Chapel Hill: University of North Carolina.

U.S. Bureau of the Census. 1979. *Statistical Abstract of the United States: 1979.* (100th edition) Washington, D.C.: U.S. Government Printing Office.

U.S. Bureau of Labor Statistics. 1948. *Worker's budgets in the United States: City families and single persons, 1946 and 1947.* Bureau of Labor Statistics, Bulletin 927.

————. 1968. *Revised equivalence scales for estimating equivalent incomes or budget costs by family type.* Bureau of Labor Statistics, Bulletin 1570-2.

U.S. Department of Agriculture, Agricultural Research Service. 1971. "Cost of raising a child." CFE (Adm.)—318. September.

————. 1982. "Updated Estimates of the Cost of Raising a Child." *Family Economics Review.* (Winter): 30-31.

U.S. Department of Health and Human Services. 1981. *Health-United States, 1981.* Public Health Service, National Center for Health Statistics. Washington, D.C.: U.S. Government Printing Office.

U.S. Department of Labor. 1982. *Monthly Labor Review,* 105 (November): 73, table 17.

van der Gaag, Jacques. 1982. "On measuring the cost of children." *Children and Youth Services Review* 4: 77-109.

Watts, Harold W. 1977. "The iso-prop index: An approach to the determination of differential poverty income thresholds." In *Improving Measures of Economic Well-Being.* Marilyn Moon and Eugene Smolensky, eds., 186-200. New York: Academic Press.

Weitzman, Lenore J. 1982. The economic consequences of divorce: An empirical study of property, alimony and child support awards. *The Family Law Reporter.* Monograph no. 5, vol. 8, no. 38: 4037-4057.